FINANCIAL DIGNITY

A PRACTICAL GUIDE TO STOP WORRYING ABOUT MONEY AND START LIVING LIFE ON YOUR TERMS

BY

ANDREAS JONES

Founder of www.wellandwealthy.org

Table of Contents

PREFACE

"The only way to be truly satisfied is to do what you believe is great work. And the only way to do great work is to love what you do." **- Steve Jobs.**

This book is a beacon of hope for those entangled in the fears and frustrations often accompanying financial decision-making. It's crafted to guide you through the murky waters of personal finance, providing a clear, actionable pathway toward economic stability and peace.

At its heart, this guide is born from a deep understanding of the common struggle against financial anxiety. This condition not only stifles personal happiness but also hampers the pursuit of one's life goals. In writing this, I drew upon my professional expertise in finance and the poignant stories of individuals I've encountered—each story echoing the need for a compassionate, practical approach to managing money.

Imagine Sarah, a young professional who juggles multiple credit card debts while striving to save for her future. Or consider John, whose dreams of starting his own business remain out of reach due to financial insecurity. Their stories are real and resonate with many, highlighting why a shift from mere survival to financial dignity is crucial.

Throughout the process of creating this book, I was inspired by the resilience and aspirations of people like Sarah and John. Their experiences underscored the need for a guide that simplifies financial principles and empowers individuals to rebuild their relationship with money.

1

Financial Dignity

I am deeply grateful for the mentors and colleagues who have shared their insights with me and the countless readers whose feedback has shaped this work into a tool for real change. Your stories and challenges have been instrumental in crafting a book that genuinely meets your needs.

This book is intended for anyone overwhelmed by financial planning or trapped in the paycheck-to-paycheck cycle. No advanced knowledge of finance is required—just a willingness to engage and apply these principles to your life.

In these pages, you will find strategies, encouragement, and inspiration to take control of your financial destiny. We'll explore practical steps to budgeting, saving, and investing, all designed to foster wealth and well-being.

Thank you for choosing to embark on this journey with me. As you turn each page, remember that every step forward is a step towards a life where your financial decisions bolster your aspirations rather than burden you. Let's begin this transformative journey to achieve economic stability and financial dignity.

Introduction

Embracing Financial Dignity - My Journey from Shame to Wellness

They say life is a rollercoaster, filled with ups, downs, and unexpected turns. My journey from financial shame, anxiety, and worry to financial wellness felt like the wildest ride of all. Picture this: each morning, I woke up with a heavy weight on my chest, drowning in a sea of student loans and maxed-out credit cards. Every bill was like a tidal wave crashing down on me, and it seemed as if the entire world expected me to have it all together. I often wondered if anyone else felt the same way. If you're nodding in recognition, then this book is for you.

I was tired of being trapped in this relentless cycle of stress and despair, unable to thrive, and living life in perpetual worry. It was time to rewrite my money story and live life on my terms. The turning point came when I learned to be kinder to myself. Instead of harsh self-criticism, I practiced understanding and patience—just like I would for a friend. This shift in self-worth turned everything around.

Now, I am dedicated to sharing my journey and the lessons I've learned. My mission is to empower you to overcome financial shame, anxiety, and worry, so you can take control of your finances, work towards financial independence, and experience financial dignity.

Financial shame runs deep. It's more than just feeling bad about money—it's a gut-wrenching sense of inadequacy and humiliation about your financial situation. Whether it's struggling with debt, living paycheck to paycheck, or wrestling with past financial mistakes, financial shame can be a heavy burden to bear alone. This emotion often stems from comparing ourselves to others or believing we've failed to meet society's expectations of financial success.

It is crucial to understand that financial shame is different from guilt. While guilt says, "I made a bad money choice," shame whispers, "I'm just bad with money." This seemingly small but significant difference can deeply impact our self-worth. Recognizing this distinction is vital for better money management.

Financial shame can drag us down, making us feel like we're not good enough and causing anxiety or even depression. This emotional struggle hinders our ability to focus on improving our finances. Yet, it's essential to remember that our worth is not tied to our bank accounts. When shame takes hold, we might avoid looking at our bank statements, spend impulsively to feel better, or miss out on opportunities due to feelings of unworthiness. Breaking free from this cycle is key to reclaiming control over our finances and boosting our self-esteem.

The effects of financial shame can infiltrate every aspect of our lives. According to the National Endowment for Financial Education, 57% of adults feel that their finances are out of control, leading to intense feelings of shame and inadequacy. This financial guilt can create a paralyzing cycle—avoiding money conversations, making impulsive financial decisions out of anxiety, experiencing increased stress, and watching relationships deteriorate under the weight of shame.

It's not about achieving perfection—it's about making progress. Ken Honda, author of "Happy Money," suggests focusing on gratitude to improve our money mindset. Developing a healthy money mindset is a journey that requires patience, continuous learning, and celebrating each small step forward. Your emotional well-being and financial future will thank you for it.

Talking about money can make us incredibly uncomfortable. I used to break into a sweat just thinking about discussing personal finances! Many of us avoid these conversations, leading to a lack of financial confidence. Did you know that only 55% of Americans feel confident in their financial knowledge? This reluctance often stems from fear of judgment, embarrassment over financial mistakes, or growing up in homes where money talk was discouraged.

Breaking the cycle of silence is essential for improving financial literacy. Start small by discussing your money concerns with trusted friends or family members. You might be surprised by how many people share your worries. Talking about money isn't about bragging or comparing—it's about learning, sharing experiences, and supporting each other on the journey to financial well-being. Let's make these discussions a part of our everyday lives!

On my path to financial dignity, I learned the importance of having a solid plan. Setting clear goals, tracking expenses, and identifying areas for improvement kept me on track. Did you know that 78% of Americans would struggle if their paycheck were delayed? Prioritizing savings, like building an emergency fund, can protect you and your family from financial instability and stress. Savings aren't just about accumulating wealth—they're about securing your peace of mind and financial future. Start building your emergency fund today and take control of your financial journey.

Embracing a new financial identity is a powerful step forward. Continue to learn about money through blogs, workshops, or seeking advice from experts. This ongoing education will equip you with strategies to manage financial stress, ease money anxiety, and conquer financial worries. Staying informed helps you make smart financial choices that align with your values and goals.

Financial dignity is a journey, not a destination. With hard work, patience, and an open mindset, we can overcome any financial challenge. By taking small steps and celebrating our successes, we can transform our relationship with money and improve our financial health. Remember, you are not alone. Your journey to financial dignity is possible, and it starts with self-compassion. You've got this!

If you're ready for a fresh start, take the leap and embrace a new financial identity. **Rewrite your money story** by reflecting on your journey, learning from your experiences, and committing to positive financial habits. Together, we can change the narrative and work towards a future where financial dignity reigns supreme. Let's rewrite those money stories!

CHAPTER 1

REDEFINING WEALTH:
BEYOND THE BANK BALANCE

The Weight of Wealth

In the quiet hum of the early afternoon, Michael sat on a worn leather chair in his sparsely furnished office, the sun casting long shadows across the wooden floor. Papers littered his desk, each sheet a testament to his financial success, but today, they seemed like mere paper. His eyes wandered to the window where a robin pecked at the ground, its movements carefree and unburdened.

Michael's thoughts drifted to his recent diagnosis. The doctor had been clear: stress was eroding his health. He needed a shift from the relentless pursuit of more money to something more decadent, something that mattered. As he pondered this new reality, the phone rang sharply, slicing through his contemplation like a knife through silk. It was an investor calling about yet another business opportunity. Michael listened half-heartedly, offering only mechanical affirmations in response.

After hanging up, he stood and walked over to the window. Outside, children played under the watchful eyes of their parents. Pure and infectious laughter filled the air. It struck him then how distant he felt from such simple joys, how his endless meetings and late nights had stolen more than time—they had sapped his vitality and peace.

He remembered his father's words whispered many years ago during a rare family dinner: "Wealth is not just what's in your bank account; it's having time for what truly brings you joy." These words now echoed in Michael's mind as he watched an elderly couple stroll hand in hand across the street, their ease with each other speaking of shared years and mutual support.

Turning away from the window, Michael made a terrifying yet vital decision—he would begin setting aside one day each week for himself. There would be no work; just time spent doing things that fed his soul: reading books left untouched on shelves, exploring nature trails once loved as a child, and reconnecting with old friends whose laughter once filled his days.

As dusk fell and painted the sky with strokes of pink and orange, Michael sat back down at his desk not to work but to write—a list not of business goals but of personal ones aimed at restoring what was truly valuable in life.

Will reclaiming time for health and happiness prove more challenging than any business deal ever was?

Wealth is More Than What is in Your Wallet

Imagine waking up each day feeling financially secure and prosperous in health and happiness. This vision is achievable and starts with redefining what wealth truly means. Traditionally, society measures wealth by the accumulation of assets and bank balances. However, this narrow focus can lead to a materially rich life but spiritually and emotionally bankrupt. It's time to embrace a more comprehensive understanding of wealth, including your physical, mental, and emotional well-being.

A Holistic Approach to Wealth

The journey toward a fulfilling life involves more than just financial prosperity. It requires a harmonious balance between your bank account and your state of mind and body. This chapter delves into the holistic approach to defining true wealth. This perspective does not diminish the importance of financial stability. Still, it emphasizes that true richness comes from a well-rounded life experience encompassing good health and emotional satisfaction.

Setting Goals for Balanced Success

Setting goals is fundamental in any growth process, but the nature of these goals significantly impacts our overall well-being. Learning to set objectives that equally prioritize financial success and personal health is crucial. We will explore strategies to achieve this balance, ensuring that one aspect of your life does not flourish at the expense of another.

Lifestyle Choices and Their Impact on Well-Being

Everyday decisions play a significant role in shaping our lives. Evaluating these choices critically helps us understand their long-term effects on our well-being. This chapter will guide you through assessing your current lifestyle choices and their impacts, paving the way for informed decisions supporting your health and wealth.

Empowering Through Knowledge

Armed with the proper knowledge and tools, you are better positioned to craft a life that reflects true wealth. Understanding the multi-dimensional nature of wealth allows you to set more fulfilling goals and make lifestyle choices that align with holistic well-being.

Actionable Advice for Real Change

Throughout this book, we offer practical advice tailored to help you effectively balance well-being with financial stability. Each chapter builds on this foundation, focusing on actionable strategies that foster economic resilience and personal satisfaction without overwhelming you.

A Year Towards a Fulfilling Life

Adopting the principles discussed here sets the stage for a transformative year—where health meets wealth, leading to a life full of satisfaction and joy. The path involves understanding complex concepts in simple terms, applying daily practical steps, and striving toward balance.

This is not merely about surviving but thriving—where each aspect of your life receives the attention it deserves. Let's embark on this journey together, fostering an environment where every individual can achieve their version of true wealth.

True wealth is not merely a number in your bank account; it's a vibrant tapestry woven from your physical health, emotional well-being, and financial security. Understanding this holistic approach is the first step towards redefining what it means to be truly wealthy.

Imagine wealth as a garden. Just as a garden requires water, sunlight, and good soil to thrive, our lives need a balance of health, happiness, and financial resources. Neglecting emotional well-being for economic growth is akin to watering only one part of the garden while letting the rest wither.

It is essential to recognize that emotional well-being and physical health are not merely bonuses but foundational elements of true wealth. Research shows that individuals who maintain a balance between these aspects are more likely to achieve sustainable and fulfilling success. This harmony helps reduce stress and enhances overall life satisfaction, reinforcing that wealth encompasses far more than financial gains.

In today's fast-paced world, it is easy to get caught up in pursuing monetary success. However, integrating wellness into our definition of wealth can lead to more meaningful achievements. By valuing mental health and physical fitness as highly as financial success, we can enrich our lives and foster a legacy of well-rounded prosperity.

Understanding wealth holistically incorporates health and emotional well-being, enhancing life's quality and sustainability.

Setting goals encompassing financial success, personal health, and happiness is crucial for a balanced life. This involves creating objectives that aim for economic growth and foster personal well-being.

Think of your life as a portfolio. Just as diversified investments help manage risk and yield better returns, a balanced set of goals that includes health, happiness, and wealth will likely lead to more stable and satisfying outcomes. This approach helps buffer against life's uncertainties and stresses by not putting all your focus on financial achievements.

Achieving this balance requires practical steps. For instance, when setting financial targets, goals should include regular physical activity, quality time with loved ones, and personal development. These goals often support each other; for example, staying physically active can improve your mental clarity and productivity at work.

It's also essential to revisit and adjust these goals regularly. What works for you at one stage may not be appropriate in another. Flexibility and adaptability are key to maintaining a balance that responds to changing circumstances.

How often do we consider the ripple effects of our goals on all aspects of our lives? For example, striving for a promotion might lead to financial gain but can also increase stress and reduce time for personal relationships.

Are your goals nurturing all areas of your life, or are they cultivating growth in one location at the expense of others?

The Holistic Wealth Framework

The Holistic Wealth Framework provides a structured way to assess and balance the three dimensions of true wealth: physical well-being, emotional wellness, and financial security. Each component plays a critical role, and their interdependence forms the backbone of a fulfilling life.

Physical Well-Being

Physical health is fundamental to overall wealth. Regular exercise, a balanced diet, and preventive healthcare contribute to longevity and quality of life, allowing us to engage in all activities fully. Consider the

Wellness Wheel, a tool that helps visualize your current health status and areas needing attention, enhancing your ability to make informed decisions about your physical well-being.

Emotional Wellness

Mental health and emotional stability are as crucial as physical health. Refer to the need to be clarified. Referrals enable us to handle stress, build strong relationships, and pursue our passions. Regular self-reflection, such as journaling or therapy, can significantly enhance our understanding and management of emotional states, contributing to a more prosperous, more balanced life.

Financial Security

While traditional definitions of wealth focus on this aspect, integrating it with health and emotional well-being offers a more sustainable approach. Financial security isn't just about accumulating wealth but also about making informed decisions that support your overall well-being, such as investing in health insurance or a retirement plan that affords you peace and stability.

These components interact continuously; for instance, better physical health can reduce medical costs, enhancing financial security. Similarly, emotional stability can lead to better decision-making and financial planning.

Over time, the dynamics of the Holistic Wealth Framework facilitate a feedback loop where improvements in one area can positively affect others. Regularly checking in on each dimension allows for adjustments that keep your life balanced and moving toward true wealth.

This framework emphasizes that true wealth is multidimensional, incorporating health, emotional well-being, and financial stability, each supporting and enhancing the others for a balanced, fulfilling life.

In redefining wealth, we've embarked on a journey that views prosperity through a wider lens. True wealth is about accumulating finances and nurturing our health and emotional well-being. This holistic approach ensures that our pursuit of financial success does not come at the cost of our happiness and health.

Throughout this chapter, we have unpacked the importance of setting goals that foster personal and financial growth. These objectives should balance our aspirations with physical and mental health, ensuring one does not undermine the other. By evaluating our lifestyle choices, we can better understand how our daily habits contribute to overall life satisfaction. This understanding is crucial as it empowers us to make informed decisions that enhance our well-being.

Takeaways and Looking Forward

Reflect on your current definitions of success and wealth. How often do they include happiness, health, and emotional fulfillment? Moving forward, let's challenge ourselves to broaden our perspectives, incorporating these essential elements into our definition of true wealth.

As we progress through the upcoming chapters, you will discover practical strategies for achieving this balanced approach. Expect to find actionable tips, step-by-step guides, and real-life examples to help you build a fulfilling life where financial prosperity and personal well-being coexist harmoniously.

Your Journey Awaits

Imagine living where you feel rich in every aspect—not just financially but also in health and happiness. This book promises to guide you towards that reality. It's about crafting a life filled with purpose and joy, where every decision you make contributes to your overall wholeness.

Stay engaged as we explore deeper into how you can apply these principles practically in your day-to-day life. Each chapter builds on the last, equipping you with the tools for lasting success and fulfillment.

Embrace this opportunity to transform your approach to wealth. The path to a balanced and blooming life is not just a dream—it's a possibility within your reach, starting today. Let's continue this journey together, fostering balance and sustainability in every step.

Reflection Questions

- How do you currently define wealth? Does it include aspects like health, happiness, and emotional well-being alongside financial success?
- Reflect on your daily routines—are they fostering a balance between your physical, emotional, and financial well-being?
- What are the long-term effects of your current lifestyle choices on your health and happiness?
- Can you recall moments when financial pursuits overshadowed your ability to enjoy life's simple pleasures? What changes can you make to prevent this from happening in the future?
- How can you diversify your personal goals to nurture all aspects of your well-being without sacrificing one for another?

Actionable Takeaways

- Redefine Wealth: Write down your personal definition of wealth, incorporating elements of health, happiness, and financial stability.
- Set Holistic Goals: Identify one specific goal each for improving your physical health, emotional wellness, and financial stability.
- Audit Your Time: Dedicate at least one day or a few hours each week to activities that recharge you emotionally and physically, such as spending time with loved ones or pursuing hobbies.
- Evaluate Lifestyle Choices: Assess one habitual decision (e.g., work hours, diet, and exercise) and determine its impact on your overall well-being. Commit to making a positive adjustment.
- Monitor Progress: Create a simple tracker to evaluate whether your efforts are supporting a balanced approach to wealth and well-being.

CHAPTER 2

PLANNING FOR PEACE: FINANCE AND MENTAL HEALTH

Can Clarity in Finances Clear the Fog of Anxiety?

In the soft light of early morning, Thomas sat at his modest kitchen table; the newspaper laid out in front of him unheeded. His mind wandered far from the inked headlines, caught in a tighter grip by numbers and deadlines that seemed to mock him from his open laptop. His fingers tapped an uneven rhythm on the wooden surface, each echoing a beat of rising anxiety that financial uncertainties often bred.

As he sifted through bills and bank statements, memories of simpler times surfaced—when his father would sit him down to discuss the importance of saving for rainy days. Those lessons felt distant now, obscured by immediate needs and unforeseen expenses that life had thrown his way. The weight of medical bills from his mother's recent illness lay heavy on his chest, a stark reminder of how quickly reserves could dwindle.

Outside, the world was waking up; birds chirped relentlessly as if to scorn his growing despair. A neighbor jogged past his window, her footsteps steady and sure—a contrast to the chaos in Thomas' mind. He envied her simplicity, her routine. Here, he grappled with figures that refused to add up while life walked outside, indifferent.

Determined not to drown in this sea of uncertainty, Thomas recalled an article about transparent financial planning. It spoke of mental relief and security—a lighthouse for those in financial fog. Could such clarity cut through his anxiety? He pondered this as he organized his documents into two piles: immediate actions and long-term planning.

The room felt cooler now as the morning aged; shadows shifted across his floor like sundials marking time's passage. As he drafted a budget with more apparent categories and set aside a fund for health emergencies inspired by past crises, something within him began to settle. It was like watching storm clouds break away to reveal clear sky stretches.

Thomas leaned back in his chair and released a breath he hadn't realized he'd been holding. The numbers on the screen looked less daunting now; they were just numbers, not monsters under the bed. With each decision towards better financial health, a small part of him healed, too.

What if everyone found such solace in transparency? Would we then walk through life's storms with steadier steps?

Unlock the Power of Peace through Financial Clarity

In a world where stress often stems from financial uncertainties, understanding the profound connection between your bank account and your mental peace is not just beneficial—it's essential. The sense of control that comes from effective financial planning can be a significant balm for the anxious mind. This chapter delves into how transparent financial strategies safeguard your economic stability and enhance your mental wellness, propelling you toward a more fulfilling life.

Financial anxiety plagues many, disrupting sleep and overshadowing daily joys with a persistent cloud of worry. However, this stress can be significantly mitigated by embracing a strategic approach to managing money, including preparing for health emergencies and unexpected expenditures. Here, we explore the relationship between financial planning and reduced mental stress, emphasizing how a well-organized financial life can lead to a more serene mental state.

Creating a financial plan might seem daunting, yet it's about setting achievable goals and taking small, consistent steps toward them. This chapter will guide you through developing simple and practical financial plans that are easy to adhere to and enjoyable. You can build wealth by establishing budgets that cater to needs and wants while indulging in guilt-free spending. This balance is crucial for long-term satisfaction and stress reduction.

Moreover, we will examine how specific financial strategies can simultaneously address economic concerns and foster mental well-being. It's about making choices that align with personal values and lifestyle preferences, which supports a healthier mindset. Implementing these strategies effectively requires understanding basic financial principles tailored to individual circumstances—an endeavor we will tackle together.

Drawing on real-life examples and actionable tips, this discussion aims to demystify the financial planning process. By breaking down complex concepts into digestible actions, you'll find clarity and confidence in your ability to manage finances. This proactive stance secures your financial future and improves your overall mental health.

The journey towards balancing well-being with wealth is ongoing and filled with learning opportunities. As we navigate these strategies together, we aim to cultivate resilience, ensuring you're prepared for whatever financial challenges may come without sacrificing your peace of mind.

Employing these insights will help transform your approach to personal finance from a source of anxiety to a foundation of peace. It's about equipping you with the tools needed for a balanced approach where health meets wealth, fostering an environment where you can thrive.

By prioritizing both aspects in harmony, the pathway to a fulfilling life becomes much more straightforward—a journey worth embarking on with enthusiasm and determination. Let's begin this vital conversation on how strategic financial planning can pave the way for wealth accumulation and enduring mental tranquility.

Understanding the Relationship between Financial Planning and Reduced Mental Stress

Financial planning is often perceived as a complex and daunting task. However, its essence is simple: to provide clarity and predictability in one's economic life. When you know your expenses, how much you need to save, and your financial goals, there's a reduced sense of uncertainty. This clarity directly affects one's mental state. Studies show that when individuals have a clear economic plan, their stress levels decrease significantly.

Imagine navigating a forest with a reliable map versus wandering without any direction. Financial planning is like having that map. It doesn't remove the forest or the walking effort but provides a sense of direction and control. This sense of control is crucial in maintaining mental calmness in the otherwise unpredictable journey of life.

The impact of financial uncertainty can be profound. It can lead to sleepless nights, anxiety, and even depression. On the other hand, a well-structured financial plan can act as a buffer against such mental stressors. It's not just about having wealth but about managing whatever resources one has effectively. This management instills a sense of personal competence and security, foundational to good mental health.

Financial literacy plays a pivotal role here. Understanding financial basics such as budgeting, investments, and savings is the first step toward effective financial planning. An informed individual is more likely to make sound financial decisions, reducing anxiety about the future. Each well-informed financial decision is a building block in the fortress that guards one's mental peace.

Understanding the link between structured financial planning and reduced mental stress is crucial. It empowers individuals to take control of their economic and mental well-being.

Developing Simple and Practical Financial Plans

Creating a financial plan you can enjoy might sound paradoxical, but it's entirely achievable. The key lies in understanding that a financial plan isn't a set of restrictive rules but a personalized strategy to ensure you can achieve your dreams without compromising your present happiness. It's about finding a balance that allows for both saving and spending in a way that brings joy and security.

Consider the process of planning a vacation. You budget the trip in advance, deciding how much to spend on flights, accommodation, and activities. This pre-planning allows you to enjoy the holiday without worrying about overspending. Similarly, a sound financial plan enables you to enjoy your daily life without guilt over expenditures, as long as they're within the boundaries of your budget.

A practical financial plan should include clear, achievable goals. Whether saving for a house, planning for retirement, or setting aside money for travel, these goals provide motivation and structure. They transform the abstract concept of saving into tangible targets that achieve a sense of accomplishment.

Flexibility is also essential. Life is unpredictable, and your financial plan should be adaptable to changes in your circumstances. This adaptability reduces the stress associated with rigid financial plans that don't allow for life's unexpected turns.

Engagement in the planning process is crucial. When actively involved in creating your financial plan, it aligns more closely with your values and lifestyle, making it easier to stick to. Tools like mobile budgeting apps can make this process interactive and fun, turning financial management from a chore into a rewarding part of your day-to-day life.

What if viewing your financial plan as a personal life strategy could transform your relationship with money?

Employing Financial Strategies for Enhanced Wellness

The Financial Wellness-Mental Health Evaluation Framework

This framework offers a systematic approach to aligning financial behavior with emotional well-being. It begins with a deep dive into one's financial literacy. Assessing one's knowledge and comfort with various financial aspects through a questionnaire sets the stage for informed financial planning.

The second step involves assessing the mental health implications of one's financial situation. Tools like stress assessment scales help pinpoint how financial pressures impact mental health. This awareness is crucial for proactively addressing financial stress.

Following these evaluations, the framework guides the formulation of a financial plan. This plan prioritizes essential expenditures for mental health resources such as therapy or wellness activities. It also emphasizes the importance of emergency savings, which provide a cushion and reduce anxiety about potential economic shocks.

The unique feature of this framework is its feedback loop. It necessitates regular revisits to the financial plan to incorporate changes in one's financial situation or emotional response to economic decisions. This continuous refinement ensures the plan remains relevant and effective in promoting monetary and mental wellness.

The interaction between the framework's components ensures that financial decisions enhance mental well-being. By evaluating financial knowledge, assessing mental stress, and continuously adapting the economic plan, the framework fosters a proactive approach to managing financial health.

Individuals can achieve a more balanced and fulfilling life by employing financial strategies that enhance economic and mental wellness.

As we wrap up our discussion on the symbiotic relationship between financial planning and mental well-being, it's clear that transparent financial planning is more than just a strategy for economic stability; it's a cornerstone for mental peace. The journey through this chapter reinforces the profound impact of well-structured financial plans on alleviating mental stress. By understanding and implementing straightforward, enjoyable financial strategies, you safeguard your wallet and fortify your mental health.

The process we've outlined here is not merely theoretical. It's a practical guide with actionable steps to improve your life significantly. Developing simple financial plans creates a buffer against life's unpredictability, reducing anxiety and stress. This isn't just about being wealthy; it's about being secure and at peace with your financial decisions, allowing you to enjoy life more fully.

Moreover, the strategies discussed are designed to be inclusive and adaptable. Whether you're a college student on your financial journey or a retiree looking to optimize your savings, these principles apply universally. They empower you to take control, make informed choices, and set realistic goals, which are essential for financial and mental wellness.

Remember, the goal here is not perfection but progress. Financial wellness is a journey involving regular assessments and adjustments. It's about finding what works best for you and adapting as your needs and circumstances change. Throughout this journey, it's crucial to remember that setbacks are part of the learning process—not failures but stepping stones to greater understanding and resilience.

Let's carry forward this mindset of empowerment and positivity. With each step you take in managing your finances wisely, you contribute to your mental peace. And remember, you're not alone in this journey. Seek advice, share your experiences, and perhaps most importantly, extend compassion to yourself through the ups and downs.

Aligning your financial actions with your values and mental health needs creates a balanced, fulfilling life. So, let's move forward with hope and determination, using the tools and insights we've gathered to build wealth and a legacy of well-being.

Reflection Questions

- How does financial uncertainty affect your mental well-being, and what small steps can you take today to address it?
- Are there any expenses in your life that cause unnecessary anxiety? How can you categorize them into immediate actions or long-term planning?
- What personal financial goals could bring you peace of mind, and how might you balance those with present-day needs and wants?
- Do you have an emergency fund or savings strategy in place for unforeseen events? If not, what steps could you take to start building one?
- What financial habits have you inherited or learned from your past, and how do they influence your current approach to money management?

Actions to Implement

- Create a Transparent Budget: Begin by dividing your expenses into two categories: immediate needs (e.g., bills, groceries) and long-term goals (e.g., savings, investments). Use a simple spreadsheet or a budgeting app to track them.
- Set Up an Emergency Fund: Start small if necessary, setting aside a portion of your income for unexpected expenses, such as medical bills or repairs.
- Educate Yourself: Improve your financial literacy by learning about basic concepts such as budgeting, savings, and investments. Take advantage of free online courses or resources.
- Reflect and Reassess Regularly: Make it a habit to review your financial plan monthly. Adjust as needed based on life changes or new priorities.
- Focus on Emotional Well-Being: Incorporate financial planning into your self-care routine by aligning it with your mental health goals. This could include allocating funds for wellness activities like therapy, fitness, or hobbies.

CHAPTER 3

UNCOVERING THE ENEMY - THE ROOT CAUSES OF YOUR FINANCIAL STRESS

When the Numbers No Longer Add Up

In the dim light of early morning, Tom sat at his kitchen table, his eyes tracing the numbers that sprawled across the bills and budget sheets before him. The steam from his coffee cup mingled with the chill autumn air sneaking through the slightly ajar window, carrying the scent of rain-soaked earth. He rubbed his temples, feeling the weight of each dollar he didn't have. It wasn't just about money, security, hope, and dreams for his family's future.

He remembered how his father used to sit at a similar table, furrowed brow illuminated by lamplight, piecing together their finances with worn-out pencils and dog-eared ledger books. Tom had promised himself then that he would find stability, that he wouldn't let uncertainty hang over his family like some relentless storm cloud. Yet here he was, a mirror image of past fears.

Outside, a leaf detached itself from an overhead branch, swirling on its descent to the wet pavement. Tom watched it momentarily before being pulled back by a new figure on his spreadsheet that refused to fit anywhere. High expenses and inadequate savings were not just terms; they were relentless waves eroding the foundations of what he'd tried to build.

Sarah entered the room quietly and noticed Tom's furrowed brows. She placed her hand gently on his shoulder—a simple touch that spoke volumes about their shared burdens and unspoken understandings.

"Maybe it's time we look into better planning or even some kind of investment," she whispered as if reading his thoughts—his worries about their children's education funds and their retirement plans echoing in her words.

Tom nodded slowly. It was not just about cutting costs but understanding where each penny went and why they could never catch up. Was it merely bad luck or something deeper within their grasp but out of sight? The day stretched out before him with tasks that now seemed trivial compared to this pressing need to reassess their financial strategy.

As Sarah brewed another pot of coffee, their home was filled with its rich aroma—a brief respite from their troubles yet a reminder of all life's simple pleasures they feared losing one by one.

How can one discern between mere misfortune and a fundamental flaw in approach when every decision feels like both an answer and a question?

Are You Being Held Hostage by Your Finances?

Welcome to the journey toward reclaiming control over your financial life and, by extension, your emotional and mental well-being. This guide begins with a crucial step: uncovering the roots of economic stress that silently undermine our sense of security and peace. Understanding these roots is not just about alleviating immediate worries; it's about laying a foundation for sustained financial dignity—a state where your finances support your values and lifestyle without causing undue strain.

Understanding Your Financial Stressors

Our exploration into financial stress begins by identifying its most common sources: high expenses and inadequate savings. These twin challenges often feed into each other, creating a cycle that can feel impossible to break. High expenses do not always arise from lavish spending; they often stem from fixed costs like housing, healthcare, or education. Meanwhile, inadequate savings may reflect insufficient income, ineffective saving strategies, or unforeseen emergencies that deplete the limited financial buffer available.

Personal Spending: A Mirror to Our Financial Health

Next, we delve into personal spending habits. This isn't about scrutinizing every coffee purchase but understanding patterns leading to financial hemorrhage. Are there recurring expenses that offer little in return? Do impulsive buys significantly toll your budget? This analysis is not meant to invoke guilt but to empower through awareness and control.

The Ripple Effects of Financial Anxiety

Acknowledging the impact of financial stress extends beyond numbers in bank accounts. It permeates all areas of life—mental health, relationships, professional growth, and physical health. Stress about finances is one of the top distractors at work and one of the most common sources of tension in relationships. By addressing the root causes of this stress, we aim to liberate not just your wallet but enhance your overall quality of life.

This chapter sets the stage for transforming financial anxiety into financial dignity. Dignity does not merely mean surviving paycheck to paycheck; it implies thriving with confidence in making informed financial decisions that align with personal goals and values.

As we move through this guide, keep in mind that each step is designed with immediacy and sustainability in mind. From reducing unnecessary expenses to improving saving strategies and simplifying investment options, every approach is crafted to help you transition from feeling overwhelmed to empowered.

Each section builds on the last, ensuring that by the end of this guide, you have a comprehensive toolkit to manage not just your finances but also the anxieties that come with them. Through practical advice, real-life examples, and actionable tips, expect to navigate your financial landscape with a new lens that focuses on opportunity rather than obstacles.

Embark on this transformative journey for economic stability, mental peace, and a dignified life where financial worries no longer dictate your happiness or self-worth. Let's move together toward understanding, action, and empowerment.

Financial anxiety is a pervasive issue that affects many individuals, often rooted in high expenses and inadequate savings. Understanding the familiar sources of this stress is vital for taking meaningful steps toward financial stability. High living costs, unexpected fees, and insufficient income can create a perfect storm of worry. It's not just about paying bills; it's about the emotional toll these pressures exert on daily life.

One significant contributor to financial anxiety is high expenses. Many people find themselves overwhelmed by the cost of necessities such as housing, utilities, transportation, and food. These essential expenses can consume a large portion of income, leaving little room for savings or discretionary spending. For instance, rent or mortgage payments often take up more than 30% of a person's monthly income, forcing them to make difficult choices between paying bills and enjoying life. This constant juggling act can lead to feelings of helplessness and frustration.

Another critical factor is inadequate savings. Even minor financial setbacks can feel catastrophic without an emergency fund or savings cushion. When unexpected costs arise—like medical bills or car repairs—individuals without savings are often left scrambling. This lack of financial security can exacerbate anxiety, creating a vicious cycle where stress leads to poor financial decision-making, further complicating the situation.

Many people struggle to understand their financial landscape. A lack of financial literacy often hinders individuals from making informed decisions about budgeting, saving, and investing. Without the knowledge to manage their money effectively, they may turn to quick fixes that provide temporary relief but fail to address the root causes of their financial stress.

It's essential to recognize that these sources of anxiety are not insurmountable. By identifying where your money goes each month and evaluating whether those expenses are crucial, you can begin to take control of your finances. Creating a budget that reflects your values and priorities can help clarify which expenses are essential and which can be trimmed back.

Inadequate savings doesn't have to be a permanent state either. Setting up automatic transfers to a savings account—even if it's just a tiny amount each month—can gradually build a safety net over time. This practice instills discipline and fosters a sense of security, alleviating some anxiety associated with living paycheck-to-paycheck.

Moreover, seeking out educational resources on personal finance can empower individuals with the knowledge to make informed decisions about their money. Workshops, online courses, or community classes provide valuable insights into budgeting, saving strategies, and investing basics—all crucial tools for combating financial anxiety.

As you work through these challenges, remember that you're not alone in your experience with financial stress. Many individuals share similar struggles, but acknowledging these issues is the first step toward transformation. Recognizing high expenses and inadequate savings as root causes allows you to strategize effectively and regain control over your finances.

Understanding Your Financial Landscape Is Key

Understanding Your Spending Habits

Financial strain often arises from a lack of awareness about personal spending habits. Many may not realize how small, seemingly insignificant purchases accumulate over time, creating a substantial financial burden. This is where taking a close look at your daily expenses becomes essential. Start by tracking your spending for at least a month. Use an app or a simple spreadsheet to record every transaction. This exercise offers invaluable insight into where your money is going and helps identify patterns contributing to stress.

Categorizing Expenses

Once you have a month's worth of data, categorize your expenses into fixed and variable costs. Fixed costs include rent or mortgage payments, utilities, and insurance—expenses that don't fluctuate much monthly. Variable costs encompass groceries, dining out, entertainment, and shopping—areas where you have more control. By categorizing your expenses, you can quickly pinpoint which areas are most straining your finances and prioritize them for review.

Identifying Problem Areas

After categorization, assess which variable expenses stand out as exceptionally high. Are you spending more on dining out than anticipated? Is there a subscription service you rarely use but still pay for monthly? Highlight these areas to gain clarity on where adjustments can be made. Understanding these details can empower you to decide where to cut back or rethink your spending choices.

Setting Realistic Goals

With clear insights into your spending habits, it's time to set realistic financial goals. For example, if dining out has become excessive, consider limiting this expense to once a week instead of multiple times. Similarly, if subscriptions are piling up, aim to cancel at least one service each month until you find the right balance for your lifestyle. Establishing specific targets helps create accountability and makes it easier to track progress over time.

The Role of Mindfulness in Spending

Mindful spending plays a crucial role in managing financial stress. This means being intentional about purchases rather than acting on impulse or habit. Before purchasing, ask yourself whether it aligns with your values and financial goals. This step can prevent unnecessary expenditures and reinforce discipline in your budget management.

Seeking Support

Sometimes, analyzing spending habits alone can feel overwhelming. Consider seeking support from friends or family who understand personal finance. Sharing your goals with someone who can hold you accountable or offer advice is beneficial. Engaging with others, whether through informal discussions or joining a financial group online, can provide fresh perspectives and encouragement.

Adapting Over Time

As life circumstances change, job changes, family growth, or unexpected expenses—so should your approach to analyzing spending habits. Regularly revisit your expense tracking process and adjust to reflect new realities in your financial landscape. Staying adaptable ensures that you remain proactive rather than reactive when managing money.

Celebrating Small Wins

Finally, celebrate the small victories along the way! When you successfully cut back on an unnecessary expense or meet a savings goal, acknowledge this achievement. Recognizing progress boosts motivation and reinforces the positive behavior changes you've made in analyzing and adjusting your spending habits.

By examining personal spending habits closely and making informed adjustments, individuals can significantly reduce their financial strain and move toward more excellent stability and confidence in their economic lives.

Financial stress can seep into every aspect of life, influencing not just bank accounts but also relationships, health, and overall well-being. When anxiety about money takes center stage, it can overshadow moments of joy and create an unbreakable cycle of worry. This pervasive nature of financial stress makes it essential to recognize its impacts so that steps can be taken to mitigate them.

The first area affected is often relationships. Financial strain can lead to conflict between partners, family members, or friends. Disagreements over spending habits or differing views on saving can create tension and misunderstandings. Open communication about finances is vital. Setting aside time to discuss financial goals can strengthen relationships and foster teamwork in managing money.

Mental health is another critical area affected by financial anxiety. Stress stemming from financial concerns can lead to feelings of inadequacy, depression, or anxiety disorders. These struggles may manifest as sleepless nights, loss of appetite, or difficulty concentrating. Recognizing these signs is an essential first step toward addressing them. Seeking support from a mental health professional can provide individuals with effective coping strategies and bolster their emotional resilience.

Health issues often arise as a consequence of chronic financial stress. The physical toll can be significant—stress may lead to high blood pressure, heart problems, or weakened immune systems. Practicing self-care becomes essential during times of financial strain. Simple activities like walking, meditating, or engaging in hobbies can provide relief and improve overall well-being.

Career performance may also suffer when one's mind is preoccupied with financial woes. Stress can diminish focus and productivity at work, leading to missed opportunities for advancement or even job loss. Setting clear boundaries between work and personal life helps maintain focus during working hours while allowing time for financial planning outside work.

Building a sense of financial awareness can counteract these negative impacts. By actively engaging with finances—tracking expenses, budgeting effectively, and setting achievable savings goals—individuals gain a sense of control that reduces anxiety. Utilizing apps or tools for personal finance management can simplify this process and clarify spending patterns.

Additionally, cultivating a strong support network cannot be overlooked. Surrounding oneself with understanding friends or joining community groups focused on financial wellness offers encouragement and valuable resources for learning new skills in managing money effectively.

Lastly, adopting a mindset centered on gratitude and forgiveness plays a pivotal role in alleviating the burdens associated with financial stress. Recognizing what one has achieved thus far—no matter how small—and forgiving oneself for past financial mistakes creates space for growth and empowerment.

In sum, understanding the wide-ranging effects of financial stress allows individuals to take proactive steps toward improvement across various life domains. By addressing these challenges head-on with practical strategies and supportive networks, it's possible to shift from feeling overwhelmed by finances to feeling empowered by choices aligned with personal values and aspirations.

Understanding the roots of your financial stress is not just about numbers on a spreadsheet; it's about reclaiming your peace of mind and crafting a path toward sustained economic health. We've explored how high expenses and inadequate savings can lead to significant anxiety and how essential it is to analyze your spending habits to pinpoint where your money is going.

Identifying these stressors is the first crucial step in developing a strategy that moves you from feeling overwhelmed to feeling empowered. It's about seeing the whole picture and recognizing that each financial decision impacts your well-being. Addressing these root causes sets the stage for a more secure and less stressful future.

Moving forward, the strategies you will learn are theoretical and practical actions you can apply today to see real change. Each chapter builds on this foundation, offering more insights into managing your finances effectively. From setting realistic budgets to understanding the psychological aspects of spending, the journey we are embarking on is designed to transform your relationship with money.

The benefits of reading this book go beyond acquiring financial knowledge. They encompass enhancing your quality of life, reducing stress, and fostering a sense of accomplishment and peace. Imagine a life where financial worries no longer weigh you down, where you have the tools to make informed decisions and the confidence to navigate unexpected financial challenges.

With each page, you'll gain more than just tips and tricks; you'll learn how to establish a mindset that embraces prudent financial planning and smart investing. This is about building a life where financial worries do not control your happiness and decisions.

As we move forward, remember that the journey to financial dignity is personal. Each step is a step toward a more secure and fulfilling life. Embrace the challenge with optimism, equip yourself with knowledge, and transform your financial stress into a foundation for lasting peace and prosperity.

Let's continue this journey together, learning and growing with each chapter as we pave the way to a life defined not by financial fear but by economic freedom and dignity.

Reflection Questions

- What are the root causes of your current financial stress?
  Identify specific areas such as high expenses, inadequate savings, or unexpected emergencies that contribute to your financial worries.
- How do your personal spending habits align with your financial goals?
  Reflect on whether your spending patterns reflect impulsive decisions or mindful choices that support your long-term objectives.
- What emotional impact does financial stress have on your relationships and overall well-being?
  Consider how financial anxiety affects your interactions, mental health, and ability to focus on daily tasks.
- What changes can you make to improve your financial literacy and decision-making?
  Identify areas where additional knowledge or tools (e.g., budgeting apps or workshops) could help you feel more confident about managing your money.
- How do your values influence your financial priorities?
  Reflect on whether your current financial strategy aligns with what you value most in life, such as security, family, or personal freedom.

Action Steps to Implement

- **Track Your Spending:** Begin logging all expenses for the next 30 days using an app, journal, or spreadsheet to gain clarity on your financial habits.
- **Categorize Your Expenses:** Divide your expenses into fixed (e.g., rent, utilities) and variable (e.g., dining, subscriptions) categories to identify areas for potential savings.
- **Set One Specific Financial Goal:** Choose a goal such as saving $100 this month, reducing dining out to once a week, or paying down a small debt. Create a step-by-step plan to achieve it.
- **Schedule a Financial Review:** Dedicate time each week to review your budget, spending patterns, and progress toward your financial goals.
- **Learn and Grow:** Commit to enhancing your financial literacy by reading a book, taking an online course, or attending a seminar on personal finance.

CHAPTER 4

BUDGETING – YOUR TICKET TO FINANCIAL LIBERATION

Can a Simple Budget Change a Life?

In the soft glow of the early morning, Emily sat at her small kitchen table, her fingers tracing the edges of a worn notebook filled with numbers and notes. The coffee machine gurgled in the background, a comforting yet mundane soundtrack to her daily ritual of budgeting. This morning felt different, though; each number was not just a figure but a stepping stone away from the tight grip of living paycheck to paycheck.

Her thoughts wandered to last Christmas when she had to decide between heating and gifts for her children. The weight of that choice still pressed cold on her chest. But today, armed with her budget, she was plotting a course towards something better—freedom. She scribbled down her expenses and subtracted them from her income, which was meticulously noted at the top of the page. The result? A small number, but positive— her first savings.

Outside, the world was waking up. A car horn blared distantly, and birds chirped their morning tunes as sunlight spilled across the linoleum floor. The aroma of fresh coffee filled the air, pulling Emily back from her reverie. She poured herself a cup and took a slow sip, feeling the warmth spread through her.

Returning to budgeting, she remembered advice from an old friend who had escaped this financial treadmill years ago. "It's not about cutting back," he had said with eyes bright with hindsight wisdom, "it's about making choices that align with your dreams." Emily smiled at this thought; it wasn't just about numbers on a page—it was about crafting life itself.

Her daughter shuffled sleepily into the kitchen—a tousle-haired reflection of hope—and tugged at Emily's sleeve, asking for breakfast. With each interaction, every decision to forego an unnecessary expense in favor of saving for future needs and desires—the school trip next spring or even just an unplanned pizza night—Emily felt more in control.

As she prepared toast and scrambled eggs for them both, she considered how each small choice was part of something much bigger than financial management; it was part of teaching her daughter about priorities and planning—a lesson far more valuable than anything money could buy directly.

As they sat eating together in comfortable silence punctuated by soft chews and clinks of cutlery against plates, Emily pondered: if budgeting could indeed be seen not as chains but as keys to unlocking potential, how might other areas in life be transformed by simply adjusting one's perspective?

Unlock Your Financial Shackles: Embrace Budgeting as a Path to Freedom

Budgeting often carries a stigma of restriction—a financial leash that many feel hinders their spending freedom. However, this perspective overlooks the profound empowerment a well-structured budget can provide. From being a mere ledger of income and expenses, budgeting is a fundamental tool that fosters financial clarity and control. By redefining budgeting as a means to financial liberation rather than limitation, we can transform our approach to personal finance and pave the way toward achieving financial dignity.

Why Budgeting Matters

In the realm of personal finance, knowledge truly is power. Understanding where your money comes from and where it goes is the first step in claiming authority over your financial future. A detailed and practical budget is not just about tracking; it's about strategically directing your resources to where they will serve you best, both now and in the future. This chapter will guide you through creating a thorough budget tailored to your financial goals and challenges.

The Freedom of Financial Control

Many people live paycheck-to-paycheck, feeling like they're just one unexpected expense away from financial disaster. This stress can be alleviated by implementing a budget that provides real-time insights into your financial status. With these insights, sudden financial shocks become less daunting as you have prepared for irregular expenses and clearly understand your financial buffer. This chapter explores how budgeting can transform your approach to money management, turning reactive spending into proactive financial planning.

Skills for Optimizing Your Financial Future

Adopting a budget is only the beginning. The true art lies in adjusting and optimizing this budget over time to align with changing priorities and goals. This process involves analyzing spending patterns, identifying wasteful expenses, and reallocating funds towards more significant investments or savings strategies. Here, we will delve into methods for fine-tuning your budget, ensuring it evolves with you and continues to meet your needs effectively.

The journey to financial liberation through budgeting is both practical and transformative. It equips you with the tools to break free from the cycle of living paycheck-to-paycheck, reduces money-related stress, and builds a foundation for lasting security and peace of mind. By embracing the principles in this chapter, you are taking an essential step toward managing and mastering your finances.

Remember, each step you take in crafting and adhering to your budget strengthens your ability to make informed decisions about your money. This empowerment is critical for achieving immediate financial goals and securing long-term economic health and dignity.

As we explore these concepts further, remember that every tip and strategy discussed here aims to enhance your understanding of money management—turning what may initially seem like constraints into powerful tools for freedom and security.

Creating a budget is a vital step toward achieving financial stability. It may seem daunting, but breaking it down into manageable steps can make the process smoother. Start by gathering all your financial information, including pay stubs, bills, bank statements, and other documents that reflect your income and expenses. This foundational step will give you a clear picture of your financial situation.

Once you have your financial data in hand, categorize your expenses. Split them into fixed costs—like rent or mortgage, utilities, and loan payments—and variable costs—such as groceries, entertainment, and dining out. Understanding these categories helps you see where your money is going each month. It's essential to be honest about your spending habits; this transparency will set the stage for making informed decisions.

Next, calculate your total income, including all sources such as salaries, bonuses, side jobs, and any passive income streams. Understanding your total earnings is essential for creating a realistic budget that aligns with your financial goals. Once you've determined your total income and expenses, subtract the expenses from your income to see how much money remains at the end of each month.

If you find yourself in the red—meaning your expenses exceed your income—take a closer look at where cuts can be made. Prioritize essential expenses over discretionary ones. For example, consider reducing dining out or canceling subscriptions that you rarely use. This isn't about depriving yourself; it's about redirecting funds to areas that matter most to you.

Creating a budget isn't just about tracking numbers; it's also an opportunity to set financial goals. Whether saving for a vacation, planning for retirement, or wanting to pay off debt faster, having specific goals gives purpose to your budgeting efforts. Write these goals down and review them regularly to stay motivated.

To keep yourself accountable, consider using budgeting tools or apps that simplify the tracking process. Many apps allow you to link bank accounts and automatically categorize transactions. This technology can save time and reduce the mental burden of manual tracking while providing real-time insights into your spending habits.

Finally, remember that budgeting is not a one-time task but an ongoing process. Life circumstances change; therefore, revisiting and adjusting your budget regularly is essential to ensure it continues to meet your needs effectively. Celebrate small wins along the way—saving a certain amount or sticking to a spending limit—as these victories will reinforce positive behavior.

Ready to Take Control of Your Finances?

Understanding Financial Control

Budgeting is essential for achieving financial control. By creating a detailed budget, you transform vague financial concerns into clear, tangible figures. Instead of feeling overwhelmed by bills and expenses, you gain clarity about where your money is going. This understanding empowers you to make informed decisions that can improve your financial health. Knowing your income and expenses enables you to prioritize spending, ensuring essential needs are covered while setting aside funds for savings and investments.

Many people perceive budgeting as a tedious exercise in restriction, but it is an opportunity for empowerment. You cultivate awareness about your financial habits by diligently tracking your income and expenses. This awareness serves as the foundation for making strategic decisions. For instance, if you notice that dining out frequently drains your budget, you can choose to cook at home more often. This shift saves money and promotes healthier eating habits, fostering a sense of overall well-being.

The Freedom of Choice

Another significant aspect of budgeting is that it enhances your freedom of choice. When you have a clear picture of your finances, you can allocate funds toward what truly matters to you. Whether saving for a vacation, investing in education, or setting aside money for emergencies, a well-structured budget allows you to plan for the future rather than merely reacting to immediate expenses. You are not just surviving from paycheck to paycheck; instead, you're actively shaping your financial destiny.

Consider the example of two individuals with similar incomes. One person lacks a budget and often feels trapped by their financial situation. They may rely on credit cards for unexpected expenses or miss opportunities for savings simply because they don't know where their money goes. The other person uses budgeting as a tool and finds ways to set aside small amounts regularly—this individual experiences peace of mind knowing they are prepared for both expected and unexpected costs.

Building Confidence

Budgeting also builds confidence in managing finances. As you become more familiar with tracking your expenses and adhering to your budget, you'll find that making financial decisions becomes easier over time. You learn the difference between wants and needs, which helps prevent impulse spending. With this newfound confidence comes the ability to easily navigate conversations about money, whether negotiating salaries or discussing bills with family members.

Moreover, budgeting fosters accountability. Sharing your budget goals with trusted friends or family can provide motivation and support as you work toward achieving them together. Knowing that someone else knows your goals makes staying committed and focused on reaching them more manageable.

A Pathway Out of Financial Anxiety

Many individuals feel trapped in cycles of financial anxiety, constantly worrying about making ends meet or facing unexpected expenses. Budgeting serves as a pathway out of this cycle by providing structure and predictability around finances. When every dollar has a purpose—going towards savings or paying off debt—you create a sense of stability that alleviates stress.

This approach doesn't eliminate challenges but equips you with the tools to face them head-on. For example, an emergency fund built through disciplined budgeting can provide security against unforeseen costs like medical bills or car repairs—knowing you're prepared diminishes anxiety.

Long-Term Benefits

The benefits of effective budgeting extend beyond immediate relief from stress; they lay the groundwork for long-term financial health. As individuals gain control over their finances through effective budgeting practices, they often find themselves in better positions for more significant financial commitments like buying homes or investing in retirement plans.

Establishing clear goals within your budget encourages a proactive approach toward saving and investing rather than reactive measures driven by fear or uncertainty. This proactive mindset opens doors to opportunities that might have been overlooked due to insufficient preparation.

Embracing Change

Ultimately, embracing budgeting as an essential tool for financial liberation leads to transformative changes in mindset and behavior surrounding money management. It shifts the perception from scarcity and limitation towards abundance and opportunity—a powerful shift that enables individuals to pursue their dreams without being hindered by financial worries.

As readers begin implementing budgeting strategies, they will likely find themselves gaining control over their finances and uncovering new possibilities that align with their values and aspirations. This newfound freedom fosters resilience against life's unpredictable nature while enhancing overall life satisfaction through informed decision-making.

Incorporating these practices into daily life may take time and effort initially, but the rewards are worth it—financial dignity is within reach. By consistently applying budgeting principles, anyone can cultivate a more secure future filled with choices rather than constraints.

B.O.S.S. Framework for Budgeting

Budgeting can be an effective way to enhance financial security and increase savings. The B.O.S.S. Framework—standing for Build, Optimize, Sustain, and Shift—provides a practical approach to creating and maintaining a budget that works for you. Each component of this framework is crucial in ensuring your budgeting process is effective and adaptable to your changing financial landscape.

Build: Establish Your Financial Baseline

The first step in the B.O.S.S. Framework is building your financial baseline. This involves identifying all sources of income, including salaries, side hustles, and any passive income streams. A complete picture of your earnings is essential before moving on to expenses.

Once you've established your income, the next task is to track all your expenses, fixed (like rent or mortgage payments) and variable (such as groceries or entertainment). Categorizing these expenses into essential needs versus discretionary spending helps illuminate areas where you can cut back. Understanding where your money goes sets the stage for making informed decisions about future spending and saving.

Optimize: Set Realistic Goals

With a clear understanding of your income and expenses, the next phase is optimization. This means setting realistic financial goals aligned with your values and priorities. Whether saving for a vacation, paying off debt, or building an emergency fund, having specific goals creates motivation and accountability.

As you set these goals, consider how they fit into your broader life objectives. Use the SMART criteria—specific, Measurable, Achievable, Relevant, and Time-bound—to ensure your goals are well-defined. This structured approach not only clarifies what you want to achieve but also helps you maintain focus as you navigate potential distractions in your financial journey.

Sustain: Monitor Your Progress Regularly

Sustainability in budgeting involves regularly monitoring your progress against those goals. This isn't just about checking numbers; it's about understanding how well you're sticking to your budget and adjusting as necessary.

Establish a monthly review process where you assess income and expenses. Look for patterns or trends that may require adjustments to spending or saving habits. Tools like budgeting apps can simplify this process by providing real-time insights into your financial flow.

Shift: Adapt to Changes

Life is unpredictable, and being flexible in your budgeting approach is vital for long-term success. The final component of the B.O.S.S. Framework focuses on shifting strategies when circumstances change, whether due to unexpected expenses or changes in income.

Budgeting isn't a static endeavor; it requires continual adaptation based on life events like job changes, family growth, or economic shifts. Maintaining an open mindset toward adjusting your budget as needed will make it easier to stay on track without feeling overwhelmed by setbacks.

Interconnected Dynamics of the Framework

The components of the B.O.S.S. Framework are interdependent; each one supports and enhances the others. For instance, optimizing goals might be unrealistic or unachievable without a solid foundation from the Build phase. Similarly, if you fail to monitor progress (Sustain), making necessary shifts becomes difficult.

This interconnectedness creates a feedback loop where each phase informs the others over time. For example, insights gained during monitoring may lead you back to adjust initial goals or spending categories.

Practical Implications

Employing this framework provides tangible benefits beyond organizing finances—it fosters an empowered mindset toward money management. By actively participating in this holistic budgeting process, individuals gain confidence in their ability to navigate financial challenges effectively.

Moreover, as habits develop around tracking spending and saving consistently, the psychological barriers associated with budgeting can diminish significantly over time.

In summary, adopting the B.O.S.S. Framework offers a structured yet flexible approach to budgeting that promotes financial security while empowering individuals on their journey toward economic freedom and dignity. Each component plays an essential role in managing finances and transforming them into tools for achieving personal aspirations and peace of mind amidst life's uncertainties.

Budgeting is often misunderstood as a form of financial restriction, but as we've explored, it's a liberating tool. You create a powerful overview of your financial landscape by systematically tracking your income and expenses. This clarity is not just about numbers; it's about taking control and making informed choices to improve your peace of mind and economic stability.

Understanding your financial flow is critical. When you know where each dollar is going, you can make adjustments that align better with your financial goals and personal values. This might mean cutting back on non-essential expenses or redirecting funds towards more rewarding investments, like education or retirement savings. The empowerment gained from this knowledge allows you to break free from living paycheck to paycheck, easing financial stress.

Moreover, the skills developed through budgeting—such as prioritizing expenses, forecasting future needs, and setting achievable financial goals—are invaluable. They provide a foundation for increased savings and enhanced economic security. Every adjustment made to your budget reinforces your path toward long-term financial freedom.

Embrace budgeting as a positive step towards managing your finances and reclaiming your life from worry and stress over money. Remember, each small step in refining your budget is a stride towards greater financial liberation. Stay committed to this process, and watch how budget control transforms into life control.

Let this chapter serve as a reminder and a guide: budgeting isn't about restriction. It's about making smarter choices that lead to a more secure and fulfilling life. Armed with these tools and insights, you are well on your way to achieving financial stability and true financial dignity. Keep pushing forward, stay informed, and remember that each day presents a new opportunity to refine your approach and enhance your financial well-being.

Reflection Questions:

- How does budgeting change your perspective on financial freedom?

  Reflect on how creating a budget could transform your view of financial control and freedom. How does it make you feel about your financial situation now and in the future?

- What financial goals would you prioritize, and why?

  After reading about the importance of setting financial goals, think about your own. What would you prioritize in your budget (savings, debt reduction, emergency funds, etc.) and why?

- How can small changes in your spending habits lead to bigger financial shifts?

  Consider the impact of reducing certain discretionary expenses (like dining out or subscriptions). How might small changes add up over time to create significant improvements in your financial health?

- What strategies will you use to stay accountable to your budget goals?

  Think about how you can keep yourself on track with your budgeting goals. Will you use apps, share your goals with a friend, or set regular check-ins to ensure you're staying committed?

- What areas in your current budget could benefit from optimization?

  Reflect on your current financial situation. Where could you adjust or reallocate funds to better meet your goals? What are the key areas that need fine-tuning for long-term success?

CHAPTER 5

CRUSHING DEBT – STRATEGIES TO BREAK FREE FROM HIGH-INTEREST BURDENS

Can Freedom Truly Begin With a Ledger?

In the dim light of early morning, Thomas sat at the small, cluttered table in his kitchen; papers spread out like a fan of fallen leaves around him. The refrigerator's hum served as a monotonous backdrop to his focused breathing. Each bill was a reminder, a call to action that he couldn't ignore any longer. The credit card statements, with their high interest rates, seemed to glare at him, taunting him with their bold figures and imminent due dates.

Thomas rubbed his temples as he looked over the numbers again. He remembered his father's stern advice about money: "It's not about how much you make but how much you keep." Those words echoed in his mind now more than ever. He dreamed of a house by the lake and mornings spent in tranquility rather than turmoil. But first, this mountain of debt demanded to be scaled.

A soft clatter came from the living room where his daughter built castles with her blocks. Her laughter pierced through the weight of his thoughts, reminding him of why this struggle was worth enduring. Thomas picked up a pencil, scribbling down potential extra payments against the highest interest debt first — the avalanche method he'd read about seemed promising. Each number was a subtraction from his bank account and a step towards liberation.

Outside, the sky brightened slowly as cars started to fill the street, people moving towards their day's labors under the soft awakening blush of dawn. Thomas knew that each had their battles, perhaps some hidden behind quiet smiles or held within clenched fists on steering wheels.

He thought about the next steps — cutting down expenses, maybe picking up freelance work on weekends — anything that could accelerate his journey to financial freedom. A sense of resolve settled over him like a cloak; it was heavy yet comforting.

As Thomas folded one statement and opened another, considering whether selling off some unused electronics could contribute to next month's payment, he wondered: Is there more peace in planning for freedom or finally achieving it?

Break the Chains of High-Interest Debt

When it comes to achieving financial freedom, prioritizing eliminating high-interest debt is more than just a strategic move—it's necessary. The weight of debts, such as those from credit cards, can suffocate your financial health, leaving you gasping for air in a sea of seemingly endless obligations. However, this chapter isn't just about highlighting problems; it's about offering you real solutions and the hope that comes with knowing you can regain control.

The Hidden Costs You're Paying

It's vital to understand that high-interest debts are not just numbers on your bank statements; they are active leaks in your financial vessel, draining resources that could otherwise enhance your life quality. Every day, these balances remain unpaid; they eat away at your potential to save, invest, and secure a comfortable future. By recognizing the actual cost of this type of debt—not just in dollars but in stress and lost opportunities—you'll see why tackling it head-on is crucial.

Mastering Effective Debt Repayment Strategies

You don't have to face this challenge unarmed. Techniques like the debt snowball and avalanche methods provide structured, practical paths to wiping out high-interest debts. These aren't just theoretical concepts but valuable tools tailored to help you clear your debts systematically. Focusing first on the most pressing debts can create momentum, like rolling a snowball downhill, growing your financial confidence as each balance is cleared.

Setting Priorities for Long-Term Relief

Understanding how to prioritize debts strategically can significantly reduce the time and money spent on interest accrual. This isn't about paying more money towards your debts; it's about paying smarter. When you know which debts to target first, you empower yourself to clear debt faster and rebuild your financial landscape more efficiently.

Each step towards conquering high-interest debt is a step towards peace of mind and economic stability. This chapter aims not just to educate but also to inspire action through straightforward guidance and real-life applications. You'll find stories of those who have successfully navigated their way out of deep debt waters, providing not only a testament to what's possible but also a blueprint for replicating their success.

The journey toward financial dignity involves addressing debts with precision and understanding their broader impacts on one's life and mental well-being. With each payment made against these high-interest obligations, one reclaims a piece of one's freedom and moves closer to a life free from the shackles of debt.

By embracing these strategies and adjusting your approach to debt repayment, you equip yourself with the knowledge needed to make informed decisions that align with long-term financial wellness goals. This chapter will guide you through this process, ensuring that the path forward is clear and achievable by the end.

Remember: every dollar saved on interest is another dollar in your pocket—freeing up resources for investments that can grow over time or securing life's various necessities without the looming shadow of debt. Start today because time is one resource we cannot recover—let's ensure every moment counts towards building a financially sound future.

High-interest debt can be a significant barrier to achieving financial well-being. Many people find themselves in a cycle of borrowing that feels impossible to escape. The allure of credit can lead individuals to accumulate balances that increase due to high interest rates. Understanding the impact of these debts on your financial health is crucial for regaining control and moving toward a more stable future.

One of the most detrimental effects of high-interest debt is its ability to consume a large portion of your income. When monthly payments are primarily allocated to interest rather than principal, it can feel like you're making no progress. This can create frustration and helplessness as your hard-earned money vanishes into fees and interest charges. The longer this cycle continues, the harder it becomes to break free, leading many into constant financial stress.

High-interest debt can also significantly limit your options in life. With so much income tied up in payments, you may struggle to save for emergencies or invest in opportunities that could improve your situation. This lack of flexibility can stifle personal growth and limit your ability to achieve long-term goals, whether buying a home, funding education or even enjoying experiences that enrich your life.

Moreover, carrying high-interest debt often takes a toll on mental health. The anxiety associated with financial instability can lead to sleepless nights and increased stress levels. You might worry about how you will make ends meet or fear unexpected expenses that could push you further into debt. This kind of mental burden affects not only your financial choices but also your overall quality of life.

Identifying the root causes of high-interest debt is essential to breaking free from its grip. Many individuals fall into this trap due to lifestyle inflation, where spending increases as income rises without corresponding savings or investments. Others may rely on credit cards as a safety net during tough times, inadvertently digging themselves deeper into a financial hole. Recognizing these patterns empowers you to make conscious changes moving forward.

It's essential to consider the long-term consequences of ignoring high-interest debt. While it may seem manageable at first glance, the compounding nature of interest means that debts can escalate quickly if left unattended. What begins as a small balance can become overwhelming over time, creating an environment where financial stability feels out of reach.

Taking action against high-interest debts requires determination and strategic planning. Acknowledge these debts' power over your finances and prioritize their elimination as a critical step towards regaining control. The sooner you confront this issue head-on, the quicker you can transition toward a healthier financial outlook.

As you reflect on the implications of high-interest debt in your life, it's crucial to remember that change is possible. By understanding its detrimental effects on your finances and mental well-being, you're already taking an important first step toward liberation from this burden.

Take Control: Your Path Forward Begins Here

Understanding the Debt Snowball and Avalanche Methods

Managing debt can feel overwhelming, especially when high-interest obligations weigh heavily on your finances. Two of the most effective strategies for tackling this burden are the debt snowball and debt avalanche methods. Each offers a structured approach to help you eliminate debts more efficiently, allowing you to regain control of your financial life.

The debt snowball method focuses on psychological momentum. It involves listing your debts from smallest to largest. You prioritize paying off the smallest debt first while making minimum payments on more significant debts. Once the smallest debt is paid off, you move to the next smallest, adding the amount you were paying on the first debt to the minimum payment of the second. This creates a "snowball" effect as you knock out debts individually. The sense of accomplishment from paying off smaller debts can be a powerful motivator, fostering a positive mindset that propels you forward.

In contrast, the debt avalanche method is about saving money on interest payments. This strategy requires listing your debts from the highest to lowest interest rate. You first focus on paying off the debt with the highest interest while making minimum payments on others. Once that debt is eliminated, you focus on the next highest interest-rate debt. This method often results in lower overall interest paid and can lead to quicker debt elimination in terms of time and cost.

Choosing between these methods depends mainly on your personal preferences and financial situation. If you're motivated by quick wins and need encouragement, the snowball method may be best for you. On the other hand, if you're more analytical and want to minimize costs over time, consider adopting the avalanche method.

Steps to Implementing Your Chosen Method

Regardless of which strategy resonates with you, implementing it requires a few straightforward steps. Start by creating a comprehensive list of all your debts, noting their balances, interest rates, and minimum monthly payments. This clarity will help you visualize what you're dealing with and set up a plan tailored to your needs.

Next, create a budget that allows you to allocate extra funds towards your chosen target debt—the smallest balance or the highest interest rate, depending on your strategy. Look for areas where you can cut back or save money each month; even minor adjustments can add up significantly.

As you progress, track each payment diligently and celebrate milestones. Whether you pay off a small balance or reach a certain percentage of overall debt reduction, recognizing these achievements reinforces positive behavior and keeps motivation high.

Staying Committed Through Challenges

While both methods are effective in their own right, it's essential to remain committed even when challenges arise. Unexpected expenses or changes in income can disrupt even the best-laid plans. If this happens, don't be discouraged—reassess your budget and make necessary adjustments without losing sight of your goals.

Consider involving accountability partners or joining support groups focused on financial wellness. Sharing experiences with others working toward financial freedom can provide additional motivation and encouragement during tough times.

Final Thoughts on Debt Reduction Techniques

Both strategies—debt snowball and avalanche—are valuable tools for breaking free from high-interest burdens. They offer structured paths toward financial freedom while accommodating different mindsets and motivations. Anyone can reclaim their financial dignity today by understanding how each method works and taking actionable steps toward implementation.

Remember that this journey is not solely about numbers; it's also about mindset transformation and reclaiming control over your life choices. As you work through your debts using these strategies, keep envisioning what life could look like without those burdens holding you back.

D.E.B.T. Management Framework

The D.E.B.T. Management Framework offers a structured method for prioritizing and eliminating high-interest debt. This approach systematically assesses one's financial obligations, focusing on creating an actionable plan that leads to financial freedom. Each component plays a crucial role in enhancing the effectiveness of debt repayment strategies, ensuring that individuals can minimize their interest costs while maximizing their progress toward financial independence.

Detailed Assessment of Current Debts

The first step in this framework is conducting a thorough assessment of all outstanding debts. This involves listing each debt, including credit cards, loans, and other financial obligations. It's essential to note the interest rates and balances owed for each item. Understanding these details allows individuals to categorize their debts effectively. This clarity sets the stage for making informed decisions about repayment strategies.

Exploring Repayment Strategies

Once debts are assessed, it's time to choose between two popular repayment methods: debt snowball and avalanche. The debt snowball method encourages individuals to focus on paying off the smallest debts first, providing psychological wins that can boost motivation. On the other hand, the avalanche method targets debts with the highest interest rates, which can save more money over time by reducing overall interest payments. Each strategy has its merits; selecting one aligns with personal preferences and financial goals.

Budget Allocation for Debt Payments

Developing a repayment plan includes identifying how much extra money can be allocated toward debt payments from monthly budgets. This process may require reviewing current expenses and finding areas where spending can be reduced. Individuals can accelerate their debt repayment efforts and reduce their total interest incurred over time by committing to consistent payments beyond the minimum amounts due.

Consolidation and Negotiation Options

As part of this framework, exploring options for debt consolidation or negotiating lower interest rates with creditors is vital. Consolidating multiple high-interest debts into a single loan with a lower rate can simplify payments and save money on interest over time. Similarly, engaging creditors to negotiate better terms can lead to more manageable payment plans that fit within one's budget.

Monitoring Progress Regularly

Regularly monitoring progress is crucial in maintaining motivation throughout the repayment journey. Individuals should celebrate milestones—such as paying off a debt or reaching specific repayment goals—to reinforce positive behavior and commitment to the process. Creating visual reminders or using financial apps can help track progress effectively.

Curbing Unnecessary Spending

Temporarily curbing unnecessary spending habits to free up resources for debt repayment is essential. This might involve evaluating lifestyle choices and identifying non-essential expenses that can be reduced or eliminated. Redirecting these funds toward debt payments accelerates progress while instilling better long-term financial habits.

Feedback Loops for Continuous Improvement

The dynamics of this framework emphasize feedback loops where monitoring results inform future actions. If specific strategies are not yielding expected results, adjustments should be made promptly. This adaptability ensures that individuals remain engaged in their journey toward financial freedom while effectively managing their high-interest debts.

By following the D.E.B.T. In the management framework, individuals gain a comprehensive understanding of their financial situation and practical tools to tackle high-interest burdens efficiently. Each step complements one another, forming an integrated approach that fosters discipline and progress toward achieving lasting financial stability and dignity.

Crushing high-interest debt is more than just a financial strategy; it is a pathway to reclaiming your peace of mind and securing your financial future. The methods discussed in this chapter, notably the debt snowball and avalanche techniques, are not just tools but lifelines that can pull you out of the depths of financial despair.

Debt, especially high-interest debt, can feel like an overwhelming burden. It consumes your income, restricts your financial options, and fuels a cycle of stress and anxiety. Recognizing this impact is the first critical step towards liberation. By prioritizing the repayment of these debts, you reduce the amount paid in interest and accelerate your journey toward financial independence.

Using the debt snowball method, where you pay off debts from smallest to largest, harnesses the psychological wins of clearing debts one by one. It's about seeing visible progress that keeps you motivated. Alternatively, the avalanche method prioritizes debts with the highest interest rates first, which can be more efficient in reducing the overall interest paid over time.

Each approach has its merits, but the key is consistency and commitment. Setting up automatic payments can help maintain discipline in repayments. Also, reassessing your budget to find extra dollars for debt can speed up the process. Every extra penny you redirect towards your debts is a step closer to financial freedom.

Moreover, it is crucial to view these strategies within the broader context of your financial health. As you reduce your debt load, you free up more of your income for savings and investments. This shift improves your current financial situation and secures your long-term financial health.

Remember, the path out of debt is a journey. It requires patience, perseverance, and, most importantly, a plan. The strategies outlined here are designed to give you control over your finances rather than letting your debts control you. Keep focused on your goals, and take it one step at a time. Your financial dignity isn't just a dream—it's within your reach, guided by informed choices and strategic actions.

As we move forward, let's carry with us the hope and the certainty that we can overcome our financial challenges. With each payment, you're not just paying off a bill but building your future.

Reflection Questions

- What is your current financial situation in terms of high-interest debt? Can you identify which debts are draining your resources the most?

- Which debt repayment method (debt snowball or debt avalanche) resonates with you more, and why? How will you implement this strategy in your own financial plan?

- Reflect on any lifestyle habits or spending patterns that may have contributed to accumulating high-interest debt. What changes can you make today to stop these patterns?

- What small, actionable step can you take this week to reduce your debt, whether it's making an extra payment or cutting back on unnecessary expenses?

- How will you stay motivated and committed to paying down your debt over time? Consider tracking your progress or setting a reward system to celebrate small wins.

CHAPTER 6

EMERGENCY FUND – YOUR FINANCIAL STRESS SAFETY NET

Can a Safety Net of Savings Untangle the Webs of Worry?

Ella sat at the small, round table by the window in her modest kitchen, her fingers tracing the rim of a half-empty coffee cup. The morning sun filtered through the gauzy curtain, casting a gentle glow on the wooden surface where an open notebook lay beside her. Pages filled with numbers and scribbles spoke of her attempts to wrestle order into her finances.

She had been up since dawn, a habit formed in quieter days when mornings offered peace before the storm of daily demands. Now, they served as a time for reflection and planning, especially after last month's unexpected medical bills threw her budget into disarray. The idea of an emergency fund had always seemed somewhat abstract, a financial adviser's cautionary tale rather than a tangible necessity—until reality proved otherwise.

Outside, the neighborhood was waking up; sounds of cars starting and distant barks punctuated her thoughts. She remembered articles read late at night about financial security, how an emergency fund wasn't just money set aside but a barrier against life's unforeseen tempests. They suggested starting small—perhaps just $1,000 to begin with—and gradually building it up to cover several months' expenses. It felt daunting yet necessary.

As she flipped through her notebook again, calculating how much she could realistically save each month from her job at the local bookstore, doubts clouded her mind. Could she really spare enough to make a difference? She imagined future crises with less sting and more solace, where money was not an immediate concern but part of a prepared plan.

Her cat, Milo, jumped onto the table, his soft paws skidding on the papers, and made his way toward Ella for his morning affection ritual. She scratched behind his ears absentmindedly while staring out at the swaying trees beyond her window. Nature seemed so adept at handling upheaval— bending in storms with resilience she longed to emulate financially.

The doorbell rang sharply, slicing through her concentration and reminding Ella that no day had waited for anyone to feel ready. Mrs. Henderson from next door probably often came by for their shared morning walk around the block—a ritual that brought normalcy and fresh air into their routines.

As she stood up to answer it, Ella thought about what achieving this first small target in her emergency fund might feel like: perhaps like seeing land after days lost at sea—a glimpse of solid ground where one could finally rest and gather strength for journeys yet unknown.

Would this early hour's resolve translate into sustained action strong enough to weave that protective net around her life?

Is Your Financial Safety Net in Place?

Imagine a world where unexpected expenses are not a source of panic but merely a minor inconvenience. This isn't a distant reality or a privilege reserved for the few; it's the achievable result of having a robust emergency fund. Emergency funds act as financial airbags, cushioning you and your family against the unforeseen blows that life inevitably delivers. In this chapter, we'll explore how crafting such a fund is not just an exercise in financial planning but a profound step toward peace of mind and financial dignity.

The Role of an Emergency Fund

The cornerstone of any solid financial strategy is undoubtedly the emergency fund. It's your first line of defense against the unpredictable nature of life. Whether it's sudden medical bills, urgent home repairs, or unexpected unemployment, these events can be destabilizing. However, with an emergency fund, you transform these potential disasters into obstacles that can be managed and overcome. Here, we appreciate its critical role in preserving your financial stability and maintaining your mental and emotional equilibrium.

Starting From Scratch

For many, the idea of saving several months' worth of expenses can seem daunting, if not impossible. But the journey to a substantial emergency fund begins with a single step: starting small. We'll discuss practical strategies to initiate this process without overwhelming you. Every little action counts towards building this essential financial buffer, from setting up automatic savings plans to identifying quick wins in your daily expenses.

Setting Realistic Targets

Understanding your personal or familial needs is crucial in defining how much you need to save in your emergency fund. Not everyone's financial demands are the same; thus, tailoring your emergency fund to reflect your specific circumstances is vital for its effectiveness. We will guide you through assessing your needs and setting realistic and achievable targets for your fund.

Building an emergency fund is fundamentally about foreseeing and preparing for life's uncertainties. It's about ensuring that when life does happen – and it will – you are ready and capable of handling it without derailing your financial health or emotional well-being.

In our discussion, we will also underscore how discipline plays a pivotal role in this aspect of financial planning. It's one thing to start an emergency fund; it's another to grow it consistently. Through examples and actionable tips, we aim to equip you with the tools needed to systematically increase your savings over time.

Lastly, our approach will be inclusive and empathetic. We will acknowledge that everyone starts from different financial standings and has different capacities for saving. By recognizing these differences, we will ensure that the advice provided is applicable and empowering for everyone, regardless of their economic background.

As we navigate through these elements, remember that the goal is not just to save money but to build a foundation upon which financial security and peace of mind rest. Let this chapter guide you in creating a safety net and a Launchpad for achieving greater economic freedom and dignity.

An emergency fund is a crucial component of financial stability. It protects against life's unexpected events, such as job loss, medical emergencies, or urgent home repairs. Many people experience anxiety when faced with financial uncertainty, often feeling trapped by their circumstances. Establishing an emergency fund can alleviate this stress, providing a sense of security that allows individuals to navigate challenges confidently.

Building an emergency fund is not just about saving money; it's about fostering a mindset of preparedness. When you have funds set aside specifically for emergencies, you're less likely to rely on credit cards or loans when the unexpected occurs. This shift can significantly reduce the financial burden and the accompanying stress. Instead of worrying about how to pay for an unforeseen expense, you can focus on solutions and recovery.

Starting small is key. You don't need to have thousands saved up immediately. Set an achievable target based on your current situation— perhaps $500 or $1,000. As you reach these smaller goals, you'll build confidence in saving and managing your finances effectively. Over time, you can gradually increase your savings goal to cover three to six months' worth of living expenses.

The impact of having an emergency fund extends beyond just financial stability; it also enhances emotional well-being. People often underestimate how much peace of mind comes from knowing a safety net exists. This reassurance allows individuals to make decisions without the constant fear of financial repercussions looming over them. Whether it's taking a new job opportunity or investing in education, having an emergency fund opens doors that might otherwise remain closed due to fear.

Moreover, an emergency fund can empower individuals to face life's uncertainties head-on. Rather than viewing unexpected expenses as insurmountable obstacles, they become manageable challenges that can be addressed without derailing one's financial health. This proactive approach transforms the relationship with money, shifting from a cycle of anxiety to one of empowerment and control.

It's essential to recognize that building an emergency fund is not merely a task but a journey toward greater financial security and independence. Each contribution to this fund represents a step away from reliance on others or high-interest debt options during tough times. This self-sufficiency fosters resilience and encourages better financial habits moving forward.

Lastly, remember that everyone's situation is unique; what works for one person may not work for another. However, understanding the fundamental role of an emergency fund in achieving financial stability is universal. A strong foundation allows flexibility and adaptability in response to life's unpredictability.

Ready To Learn How To Start Building Your Own Safety Net?

Understanding the Importance of Starting an Emergency Fund

Building an emergency fund can feel daunting, especially when financial challenges loom large. However, starting small can make this process more manageable. Begin with a specific, achievable goal. This could be as simple as saving $500 or $1,000. Setting a clear target gives you something concrete to work towards and provides motivation as you see your savings grow.

Once you've established your initial goal, creating a plan for consistent contributions is essential. This doesn't mean you need to sacrifice all your discretionary spending; instead, look for minor adjustments in your budget that can free up funds for your emergency fund. Consider setting aside a percentage of each paycheck or directing any unexpected windfalls—like tax refunds or bonuses—straight into your savings.

Automate Your Savings

One effective way to build your emergency fund is through automation. Set up automatic transfers from your checking account to your savings account right after you receive your paycheck. This way, you treat savings like any other bill that needs to be paid each month. Automating the process removes the temptation to spend that money elsewhere and ensures consistent growth in your fund.

In addition to automation, utilize high-yield savings or money market accounts for your emergency fund. These accounts typically offer better interest rates than traditional savings accounts, which means your money can work harder for you while remaining easily accessible in times of need.

Track Your Progress

As you contribute to your emergency fund, keep track of your progress regularly. Visual aids like charts or apps can help you see how far you've come and encourage continued saving behavior. Celebrating small milestones can also boost motivation and reinforce positive habits.

If life gets in the way and you are dipping into the fund, don't be too hard on yourself. Unexpected expenses are part of life; what's important is how you respond afterward. Plan to replenish what you've used and continue building toward that initial goal.

Be Flexible and Adjust Your Goals

Financial situations can change due to various factors such as job loss, medical emergencies, or unexpected expenses like car repairs. Therefore, it's crucial to remain flexible with your goals. If needed, adjust the amount you're saving based on changes in income or expenses without abandoning the idea of an emergency fund altogether.

Remember, even incremental progress matters. If you cannot meet your target one month due to unforeseen circumstances, recommit to saving as soon as possible rather than giving up entirely.

Create a Supportive Environment

Surrounding yourself with supportive individuals can also bolster your efforts to build an emergency fund. Share your goals with family members or friends who understand the importance of financial security. They can provide encouragement and accountability while offering tips based on their experiences.

Furthermore, consider joining online communities focused on personal finance where members share their stories and strategies for saving effectively. Engaging with others on similar paths can provide motivation and new ideas for reaching financial goals.

The Power of Mindset

Lastly, it's crucial to cultivate a positive mindset about saving money and building an emergency fund. Recognize that every dollar saved is closer to financial stability and peace of mind. Changing how you view saving— from a burden to an empowering action—can transform how effectively you build your fund.

By adopting these strategies—starting small, automating savings, tracking progress, being flexible with goals, creating a supportive environment, and maintaining a positive mindset—you will be well-equipped to establish an adequate emergency fund that acts not only as a financial safety net but also alleviates the stress associated with unexpected expenses. Your journey toward financial security begins here; take those first steps today!

E.F.F.O.R.T. Framework for Emergency Fund Targets

Setting realistic targets for your emergency fund is essential in creating a financial buffer to ease stress and provide peace of mind. The E.F.F.O.R.T. framework is designed to guide you through evaluating and establishing an emergency fund that meets your personal and familial needs.

Evaluate Your Expenses

The first step in this framework is to evaluate your expenses. Understanding your monthly costs allows you to determine how much money you'll need to save. List all essential living expenses, such as housing, utilities, groceries, transportation, and healthcare. Once you have this information, calculate the total amount required for three to six months' expenses. This baseline will serve as the foundation for your emergency fund target.

Formulate Incremental Goals

Next, it's essential to formulate incremental goals that break down your larger target into manageable milestones. Instead of feeling overwhelmed by the total amount needed for your emergency fund, set smaller, specific savings targets. For instance, if you aim to save $6,000 over a year, aim to contribute $500 monthly or about $250 biweekly. These incremental goals help maintain motivation and provide a clear path toward achieving the larger target.

Focus on Automatic Savings

Focus on automatic savings strategies to build your emergency fund effectively. Setting up automatic transfers from your checking account to a dedicated savings account can make saving feel effortless. Treat these contributions like regular bill payments—non-negotiable and essential.

Automating this process reduces the temptation to spend that money elsewhere while ensuring consistent progress toward your goal.

Optimize Accessibility

Your emergency fund should remain accessible yet distinct from everyday spending accounts. Choose a savings vehicle that offers interest but limits easy access—this helps prevent impulsive withdrawals for non-emergencies. Online high-yield savings accounts are often a good option as they provide better interest rates while keeping funds separate from daily finances.

Recognize When to Use It

Understanding when it's appropriate to tap into the emergency fund is crucial for maintaining its integrity. This fund is designed for unexpected expenses such as medical emergencies or job loss—not for planned purchases or minor inconveniences. Being clear about these scenarios reinforces the fund's purpose and keeps it intact for emergencies.

Track Progress and Adjust

As you work towards building your emergency fund, regularly track progress and adjust as necessary. Life circumstances change—unexpected expenses may arise, or income may fluctuate—affecting how much you can save each month. Periodically reassess your goals based on current financial conditions and adjust accordingly without losing sight of the overall target.

Teach Financial Resilience

Finally, it's important to teach financial resilience within families or communities. Encourage discussions about budgeting, saving habits, and the importance of having an emergency fund with family members or friends who may also be struggling with financial anxiety. Sharing knowledge fosters a supportive environment where everyone feels empowered to take control of their finances.

The E.F.F.O.R.T. framework provides a structured approach to setting realistic targets for an emergency fund and highlights its role in alleviating financial stress over time. By systematically working through each component, individuals can create a safety net that contributes significantly to their overall well-being while instilling confidence in their ability to manage unexpected challenges.

An emergency fund is not merely a financial strategy; it's a cornerstone of peace of mind. Throughout this chapter, we've explored how establishing such a fund is essential for anyone looking to secure their financial future and alleviate stress. Remember, the goal here is to save money and build a buffer that shields you and your family from unexpected economic downturns.

Start small and stay consistent. Begin with a manageable goal, perhaps the cost of a single month's living expenses, and gradually increase this as your savings muscle strengthens. This approach makes the task seem less daunting and encourages a habit of saving that can benefit all areas of your financial life.

Tailor your funds to your needs. In financial planning, one size does not fit all. Consider your particular circumstances—be it job security, health, or family responsibilities—and set your emergency fund targets accordingly. This personalized strategy ensures that you are adequately covered for the kinds of emergencies most likely to occur in your life.

Remember, an emergency fund serves as your financial stress safety net, catching you and your loved ones in times of need without the additional worry of monetary instability. By taking proactive steps today, you're not just planning financially but also investing in your mental well-being and future serenity.

Let this be a call to action: begin today, no matter how small the initial step might seem. Every contribution to your emergency fund is a step away from financial anxiety and a step towards lasting peace and security. Adopting a disciplined approach to building and maintaining this fund empowers you to face unforeseen challenges confidently and calmly.

Lastly, let gratitude be a part of this journey. Be grateful for each opportunity to save, for each dollar added, knowing that you are fortifying your future against uncertainty. This mindset enriches your financial health and enhances your overall outlook on life.

With these strategies, tools, and mindsets, you are well on your way to transcending the anxieties tied to financial uncertainties. Forge ahead with resolve and optimism, and let each step reinforce your path toward a more secure and dignified financial future.

Reflection Questions

- What is the current state of your financial safety net, and how prepared do you feel to handle unexpected expenses?

  Consider whether you already have an emergency fund, how much you've saved, and what areas you might need to improve to feel more secure.

- How can you apply the E.F.F.O.R.T. framework (Evaluate, Formulate, Focus, Optimize, Recognize, and Track) to set achievable targets for your emergency fund?

  Reflect on the steps you could take today to start building or enhancing your emergency fund using this approach.

- What is one small, realistic savings goal you could set to begin building your emergency fund?

  Think about how much you can comfortably set aside each month and how you will track and adjust this goal over time.

- How can automating your savings contribute to building your emergency fund with less effort and stress?

  Reflect on the automatic savings methods available to you and how they could help you consistently save without feeling overwhelmed.

- What changes in your mindset could help you view building an emergency fund as an empowering, rather than burdensome, task?

  Consider how you can shift your perspective on saving, focusing on the peace of mind it brings instead of feeling restricted by it.

CHAPTER 7

DEBUNKING THE HUSTLE MYTH: PRODUCTIVITY VS. HOURS

Can the Clock Measure Success?

In the amber glow of a late afternoon, Thomas shuffled papers across his desk with a sigh that seemed to carry the day's weight. The office around him buzzed with the quiet hum of computers and the distant murmur of colleagues discussing their weekend plans. He had stayed late again, missing another of his son's soccer games—a fact that sat in his stomach like a stone.

Thomas had always believed in the power of hard work. His father, a stern man with calloused hands and sharp eyes, had taught him that relentless effort and long hours earned him success. Lately, however, each additional hour at the office has dimmed his vigor rather than brightened his prospects. His hands paused on a report, his mind wandering to last Tuesday when he had collapsed into bed only to be haunted by a relentless ticking clock in his dreams.

Across from Thomas, Janet packed her bag, her movements quick but precise. "You know," she started, pausing by his desk, her voice dropping to a conspiratorial whisper, "I read somewhere that working too much can make you less productive."

The words hung in the air between them like smoke. Could there be truth to it? He pondered this as he watched her leave, her steps light and sure.

As he turned back to his computer screen, Thomas let his mind drift to an article he had skimmed on efficient working practices. It spoke of balance and health—words that seemed foreign yet tantalizingly within reach. What if he could change? What if success wasn't measured by hours but by well-being and output?

A gentle breeze fluttered through an open window, carrying the scent of rain-soaked earth from the garden below—an aroma that reminded him of childhood afternoons spent outdoors rather than indoors. It nudged him towards thoughts of tomorrow; perhaps it was time to leave earlier and spend some moments under the vast sky before dinner.

As Thomas gathered his things slowly—his movements not hurried but thoughtful—he wondered what might await him if he stepped away from old beliefs. Could there be more success in less striving?

Is it possible that stepping back could bring us closer to what we seek?

Is Hustling Harder Truly the Road to Success?

The pervasive mantra of our modern work culture seems to be, "The more hours you put in, the more successful you will be." Yet evidence is mounting against this notion, suggesting that relentless overworking might hinder productivity and personal well-being. In an era where the hustle is often glorified, it's crucial to dissect whether these extended hours propel us toward success or set us up for a downfall.

The Myth of More Equals More

At first glance, logging extra hours at work seems like a straightforward path to increased output and career advancement. However, this approach fails to account for the law of diminishing returns regarding human performance. Research consistently shows that productivity plateaus and then declines after a certain point. This chapter explores how sustained overworking detrimentally impacts personal health and workplace efficiency.

Efficient Practices over Extended Hours

Identifying work practices that maximize efficiency without necessitating longer hours is essential. Techniques such as task prioritization, strategic breaks, and leveraging technology can amplify productivity without additional strain. Individuals can achieve more in less time by focusing on efficiency rather than duration, leaving room for recovery and personal pursuits that enhance overall life satisfaction.

The Role of Rest in Productivity

Contrary to the hustle culture's narrative, rest is not an opponent but a partner to productivity. Integrating sufficient downtime into one's schedule is crucial for maintaining long-term productivity. This segment will discuss strategies for embedding rest and recovery within busy lifestyles, ensuring that both mind and body remain fit for peak performance.

A Balanced Approach for Sustained Success

Adopting a balanced approach is essential not just for individual well-being but also for sustained business success. Companies and professionals must recognize the importance of mental health and its direct impact on output quality and employee retention. This chapter will provide actionable steps toward creating a balanced routine supporting professional goals and personal health.

By reevaluating our work habits through the lens of well-being and wealth creation, we can redefine what true success looks like today. It's about crafting a fulfilling life where health meets wealth, starting from day one. Adopting more brilliant work strategies while respecting our human limits sets the foundation for thriving businesses and enriched lives.

In essence, debunking the hustle myth isn't about working less—it's about working right. As we progress through this exploration, remember that sustainable productivity combines clever work tactics and ample rejuvenation—a harmonious balance that fosters wealth and well-being.

The Hidden Costs of Overworking

Overworking seems like a quick path to success, but it often leads to severe personal health issues. Studies indicate that individuals who consistently work extended hours are at a higher risk of developing heart disease, stress-related illnesses, and mental health problems such as anxiety and depression. The toll on one's health can be substantial, translating into decreased productivity both in quality and output.

Imagine a car being pushed beyond its limits without regular maintenance. Initially, it may operate fine, but over time, the wear and tear will lead to breakdowns that could have been avoided with proper care. Similarly, when we overwork ourselves, we might keep up for a while, but eventually, our health deteriorates, affecting our work performance.

Workplace studies show that overworking decreases cognitive function, affecting critical thinking, creativity, and problem-solving skills. This impacts the quality of work produced and increases the likelihood of mistakes, which can be costly. In the long run, this diminishes overall workplace productivity, contrary to the intended goal of working more hours.

Moreover, overworked employees often experience burnout, resulting in high company turnover rates. This affects team morale and increases the costs associated with training new employees. Thus, the cycle of overworking can create a less efficient, more stressed workplace environment.

Contrary to popular belief, overworking leads to significant health issues and reduces overall productivity.

Efficient Practices for Enhanced Output

What if you could achieve more in less time? Efficient work practices are key to maximizing productivity without needing overtime. Research shows that strategic breaks, proper task delegation, and the use of technology can significantly boost efficiency.

For instance, the Pomodoro Technique, where work is broken down into intervals with short breaks, improves focus and maintains consistent performance throughout the day. This method helps manage time effectively and ensures that energy levels are balanced.

Rhetorical question: Have you ever noticed how a well-rested mind is often the most creative? It's not about the number of hours you put in but the quality of those hours. Implementing efficient work practices can lead to a more productive and fulfilling workday.

Another effective practice is setting clear, achievable goals. This helps prioritize tasks and reduces time spent on unnecessary activities. By focusing on what truly matters, you can enhance your output significantly without extending work hours.

Consider the analogy of a gardener who focuses on watering the most fruitful plants; concentrating resources on the most promising areas maximizes the overall yield. Similarly, focusing your efforts on the most impactful tasks can lead to better results in shorter periods.

Can adopting these efficient work practices be the key to achieving more while working less?

Integrating Rest into Busy Schedules

Incorporating sufficient rest and recuperation into one's schedule is essential for maintaining productivity. Just like machines need downtime for maintenance, our bodies and minds require rest to function optimally. Ignoring this need can lead to burnout and decreased efficiency over time.

The research underscores the importance of quality sleep and regular daily breaks to sustain high cognitive function and creativity levels. It's not just about the quantity of work but also the quality, which is significantly enhanced by rest.

Imagine a bow constantly strung tight, never relaxing. Eventually, the tension would damage the bow. Similarly, without adequate rest, our ability to perform at our best diminishes, and we risk long-term health problems.

A practical step for integrating rest into a busy schedule is to start small; even short breaks during the day can rejuvenate the mind and improve focus. Gradually, these breaks can become a natural part of your daily routine, ensuring you remain productive without compromising your health.

By understanding the importance of rest, adopting efficient work practices, and recognizing the detrimental effects of overworking, we can achieve a balanced and productive life.

The Time-Optimized Productivity Plan

In debunking the hustle myth, we've established that prolonged hours do not equate to increased success. Instead, they often lead to diminished productivity and potential health issues. To counter this, a structured, actionable process is essential. This plan helps maintain high productivity without overworking and integrates well-being into your daily routine.

Step 1: Self-Assessment

Begin with a detailed log of your daily activities for one week. Record the time spent on work tasks versus breaks and personal activities. This self-assessment will highlight how your hours are distributed and where changes are needed.

Step 2: Identify Peak Productivity Times

Monitor when you feel most energetic and focused during the day. Everyone has different peak times; identifying yours will help you schedule tasks when you are most efficient.

Step 3: Prioritize Tasks Using the Eisenhower Matrix

Categorize tasks into urgent, important, less urgent, and less critical. This prioritization helps focus on what truly matters without wasting energy on low-priority activities.

Step 4: Structured Scheduling

Create a schedule with time blocks for focused work followed by short breaks. For instance, the Pomodoro Technique suggests 25-minute work intervals followed by 5-minute breaks, enhancing concentration and reducing fatigue.

Step 5: Regular Physical and Relaxation Activities

Incorporate yoga, meditation, or brisk walking into your weekly schedule. Regular physical activity and relaxation practices are crucial for long-term productivity and well-being.

Evaluation and Adjustment

Review your productivity and well-being regularly. Adjust your schedule to find what best suits your personal and professional life balance.

This process should be initiated over a month to allow habits to form and effects to be noticeable. Remember, the goal is to work smarter and live a balanced life where productivity and well-being coexist harmoniously.

By embracing these steps, you empower yourself to achieve sustained productivity without compromising your health. This approach enhances your output and improves your overall quality of life. As we move forward, let's carry these principles with us, fostering environments where health and productivity support one another in a balanced manner.

Reflection Questions

- How do you currently define success? Do you associate it more with the number of hours worked or the quality of work and personal well-being?
- Can you identify any patterns in your work habits that contribute to stress or burnout? What changes can you make to shift from quantity to quality in your workday?
- Think about your peak productivity times. How can you structure your day to focus on your most important tasks during these periods?
- What are some small steps you can take to incorporate rest into your daily routine to maintain a sustainable work-life balance?
- Reflect on a time when you felt overworked but didn't see the desired results. How might implementing strategies like task prioritization or strategic breaks have improved your outcome?

CHAPTER 8

THE CLARITY CONNECTION: THIS FUELS WEALTH

Can Good Health Truly Shape Financial Futures?

Marian stood at her small, cluttered office window, watching the rain drizzle against the pane. It was a grey Tuesday morning, and the rhythmic pattern seemed to echo her feelings of monotony and fatigue. Lately, her job as a financial advisor had felt more like wading through a swamp than navigating clear waters. She knew something needed to change.

Her mind wandered back to the wellness seminar she had attended the previous weekend, where a speaker had emphasized the connection between good health and effective decision-making. "Stress clouds judgment," the speaker had said, "and poor health diminishes our ability to handle financial challenges." Marian had nodded along then, but now those words played on repeat in her head as she considered her relentless headaches and sleepless nights.

She turned from the window and glanced at her desk, piled high with client files and half-finished cups of cold coffee. The room smelled faintly of old paper and stale air—starkly contrasting the fresh pine scent that had filled the seminar space. She remembered feeling more alive there, more capable. Could it be that her declining physical health clouded her professional judgment?

Marian's thoughts were interrupted by a soft knock on her door as she sifted through a file, trying to prepare for an upcoming client meeting. It was her colleague, Jake. He peered in with concern in his eyes.

"Hey, Marian," he said gently. "You've been cooped up in here all morning. Want to take a walk? Get some fresh air?"

Marian hesitated for only a moment before nodding gratefully. As they walked down the quiet street lined with budding trees and soft breezes that swept away some of her mental fog, Jake listened intently as Marian voiced her concerns about how stress might affect her work performance.

"You know," Jake mused as they paused at a corner, waiting for the light to change, "maybe it's not just about managing stress but actively improving our overall health—physically and mentally—to make better decisions."

The light turned green, and they crossed together in thoughtful silence until they reached a small park bench overlooking a pond where ducks floated serenely.

Sitting beside him, Marian felt a slight sense of peace settle over her like sunshine breaking through clouds after rain—subtle yet profound.

Could prioritizing well-being be the key to unlocking better financial outcomes for herself and her clients?

Is it possible that by caring for ourselves, we can better manage our finances and all aspects of our lives?

Unveiling the Hidden Link: How Your Health Directly Influences Your Wealth

The delicate balance between well-being and financial security lies at the heart of a fulfilling life. Too often, we overlook how closely these elements are intertwined, particularly how our physical and mental health can profoundly impact our financial decision-making. This chapter delves into the critical understanding that maintaining optimal health is not just a matter of personal well-being but is directly connected to achieving clearer, more effective financial outcomes.

Stress and poor health are not merely discomforts—they are barriers that can cloud judgment and reduce our ability to make sound financial decisions. When stressed, our minds are preoccupied with immediate concerns, often neglecting long-term planning and rational analysis, which are crucial in managing finances. Here, we explore the direct correlation between reduced stress levels, better health, and enhanced financial decision-making capabilities.

The Power of Clarity in Financial Decisions

One of the essential insights we will uncover is how stress directly influences our cognitive functions. It's not just about feeling better; it's about performing better—especially when it comes to tasks that require high levels of cognition, such as financial planning and investment choices. By understanding this link, we can use targeted health strategies to improve our mental clarity and economic understanding.

Transformative Health Strategies for Financial Success

Learning practical techniques to maintain good health and boost decision-making prowess forms a core part of our discussion. These strategies are not complex medical regimens but simple, implementable lifestyle adjustments that can significantly improve how we handle financial matters. Whether it's regular physical activity, improved nutrition, or mindfulness practices, each enhances our cognitive function.

Practical Steps toward a Healthier Financial Future

Moreover, effectively applying these health strategies requires more than just knowledge; it demands action. This segment guides you through setting realistic goals and systematically integrating these health practices into your daily routine for clearer thinking. The focus is on actionable steps that align health improvement and financial strategies to work together toward a more prosperous future.

Empathy for personal struggles with stress and its impact on finances will be woven throughout this narrative. It's vital to approach this topic compassionately and understand that everyone's journey is unique. Acknowledging diverse experiences and challenges aims to make this guidance as inclusive and applicable as possible.

To sum up, prioritizing your health is not just about living longer—it's also about living better, especially regarding your financial well-being. Through practical advice and real-life applications, this chapter aims to equip you with the tools needed for making informed decisions where your health supports your wealth.

Understanding the Impact of Stress and Health on Financial Decisions

Studies have consistently shown that stress can significantly impact our cognitive functions, including memory, attention, and decision-making. Specifically, when stressed, our bodies are in a 'fight or flight' mode, which is not conducive to the thoughtful, deliberate decision-making required to manage finances. This heightened state can lead to impulsive decisions, often with a short-term focus that neglects long-term consequences.

Imagine trying to read a complex financial report in the middle of a noisy, chaotic room. Just as external noise can disrupt your concentration, internal stress creates a mental cacophony, making it difficult to focus on the task. This analogy highlights how stress can cloud our judgment, affecting our financial clarity.

Conversely, good health acts as a bedrock for sound decision-making. A well-rested, nourished, and calm mind is much better equipped to assess financial risks and opportunities, plan for future needs, and make decisions that align with long-term goals. This is not just theoretical— numerous studies link good health with improved cognitive function and better financial outcomes.

Healthier individuals tend to have lower healthcare costs, translating into more savings and less financial stress. Additionally, when you feel good physically, you're more likely to feel optimistic and in control, which is beneficial when making financial decisions. It's a virtuous cycle: good health supports sound financial decisions, which can lead to less stress and better overall health.

Managing stress and maintaining good health are crucial for financial clarity and sound decision-making.

Techniques to Enhance Decision-Making through Health

Maintaining a balanced diet, regular exercise, and adequate sleep are foundational to good health. These are good for your body and investments in your cognitive capital. For instance, exercise increases blood flow to the brain, which can help enhance your problem-solving abilities and memory.

Isn't it fascinating to think of your brain as a bank where health deposits contribute to wealth withdrawals? As you would invest in high-quality stocks for financial gain, investing in your health yields dividends through clearer thinking and better decision-making.

Furthermore, mindfulness and meditation have been shown to reduce stress and improve concentration. These practices help clear the mind of clutter, allowing for more focused thought processes, essential when handling complex financial matters. Incorporating these techniques into your daily routine can be as simple as dedicating a few minutes daily to quiet reflection.

Stress management should also be a priority. Identifying sources of stress and developing coping strategies can prevent stress from overwhelming your cognitive functions. Techniques might include setting clear boundaries at work, seeking social support, and engaging in hobbies you enjoy.

A practical step-by-step approach to integrating these health techniques could be the following:

- Start with a small, manageable goal, such as a 10-minute daily walk.
- Gradually incorporate additional elements like balanced meals and mindfulness exercises.
- Regularly assess your stress levels and adjust your strategies as needed.

Could recognizing and investing in your health be the key to unlocking your financial potential?

Applying Health Strategies for Financial Clarity

Optimal health can lead to clearer thinking, essential for making sound financial decisions. Applying health strategies effectively means integrating habits into your daily life that bolster your physical and mental well-being.

Consider the scenario of a busy professional integrating short meditation sessions into their morning routine. Over time, they notice a significant improvement in focus and reduced impulsive spending. By improving mental clarity, this simple change helps make more considered financial choices.

Eating well is another powerful strategy. Nutritious foods fuel the brain, enhancing cognitive functions necessary for financial planning and decision-making. Imagine your body as a high-performance vehicle;

premium fuel will ensure it runs smoothly and efficiently, avoiding breakdowns that could impede your journey toward financial stability.

Regular physical activity is equally important. It boosts overall health and has been directly linked to improved brain function. Activities like yoga and walking can also reduce stress levels, making it easier to approach financial decisions calmly and clearly.

Adopting these health strategies can enhance your ability to think clearly and make decisions that will positively impact your financial well-being.

By understanding how stress affects financial decisions, learning health maintenance techniques, and applying these strategies, we can enhance our cognitive function, leading to clearer thinking and better economic outcomes.

Throughout this chapter, we've explored the undeniable link between well-being and wealth management. Understanding how stress and health impact financial decisions is not just theoretical; it's a practical, everyday reality that affects us all. By implementing strategies to maintain optimal health, we directly enhance our ability to make more precise, more effective financial choices.

We must recognize that our mental clarity and physical health are passive background factors and active players in our financial success. The techniques discussed here are more than just good health practices; they are critical tools for improving our decision-making capabilities in economic matters. Each step towards better health can be seen as better financial stability.

Remember, the journey towards improved well-being with an eye on financial clarity isn't about making monumental changes overnight. It's about tiny, manageable adjustments that collectively make a significant impact. For instance, incorporating regular physical activity or mindfulness exercises into your routine can dramatically reduce stress levels, enhancing mental clarity and decision-making prowess.

Moreover, applying these health strategies consistently will help establish a strong foundation for clearer thinking. This isn't just beneficial for your financial decisions; it's a holistic improvement that touches every aspect of life. From handling daily expenses more judiciously to making long-term investment choices more strategically, the benefits of this approach are comprehensive and far-reaching.

Let's also remember that every individual's situation is unique, and thus, flexibility in applying these principles is key. What works for one person might need adjustment for another. This personalized approach ensures that the strategies you adopt are effective and sustainable in the long term.

By now, it's clear that the interplay between health and wealth is more than just a coincidence—it's a powerful synergy that, when harnessed, can lead to a more prosperous and fulfilling life. As you move forward, keep these insights in mind, adapt them to your circumstances, and watch as they positively change your well-being and financial outcomes.

Let this knowledge empower you to make informed, confident decisions that pave the way for a balanced, thriving existence where well-being and wealth go hand in hand.

Reflection Questions

- **Health and Decision-Making:** Reflect on a recent financial decision you've made. How did your physical and mental well-being influence the clarity of your judgment? What might have been different if you had been feeling healthier and less stressed?
- **Stress Management:** Consider the stress factors in your life. How can you incorporate stress-reducing practices (like exercise, nutrition, or mindfulness) into your routine to improve both your health and financial decisions?
- **Health as an Investment:** In what ways can you view your health as an investment that directly impacts your financial success? What specific changes can you make to prioritize your health, knowing that it will improve your ability to make sound financial decisions?
- **Setting Realistic Goals:** What are some small, achievable health goals you can set this week that could lead to greater clarity in your financial decision-making? How will you track your progress to ensure these health habits stick?
- **Long-Term Benefits:** How can you apply the understanding that a healthier body and mind lead to better long-term financial outcomes? What steps will you take today to start integrating healthier habits into your life for future financial clarity?

CHAPTER 9

LITTLE CHANGES, BIG OUTCOMES: KEEP IT SIMPLE

Can Small Steps Truly Transform?

Amelia walked through the park, her feet brushing softly against the fallen leaves of early autumn. The crisp air filled her lungs, each breath a silent reminder of the simple joys she often missed in her relentless pursuit of success. Lately, her life had become a blur of meetings and deadlines, a high-stress symphony that played on an endless loop.

As she walked, Amelia's thoughts turned inward. She recalled a conversation with an old friend who had suggested integrating small health practices into her daily routine. "It's not about overhauling your life," he had said, his voice a calm contrast to the storm in her mind. "It's about weaving little moments of peace and wellness into what you already do."

She remembered how she used to meditate in the mornings, how those few minutes of silence seemed to expand time, giving her more than they took. Now, those practices felt like distant memories, lost amidst the demands of her career.

A child's laughter pulled her from her reverie. Nearby, a young mother played hide-and-seek with her son among the golden trees. Amelia watched them for a moment, their joy infectious. It struck her how they found such immense happiness in such simple play; it was all about being present.

Turning back on her path, she decided to reclaim those small practices. Maybe she could start again with just five minutes of meditation each morning or take these walks more regularly. Each step felt lighter, as if by deciding she had already lifted some weight from her shoulders.

As Amelia neared the end of the park path and prepared to re-enter the rush of city streets, she wondered: If small steps can lead to significant changes in well-being, what might happen if everyone found their way to weave health into daily life?

Small Steps to Big Well-being Gains

Imagine effortlessly weaving wellness into the fabric of your daily life, where tiny changes ripple out to manifest significant benefits. This vision is achievable and essential for anyone striving to marry health with wealth in pursuit of a fulfilling life. In our fast-paced world, integrating small, manageable health practices into our day-to-day routines can be surprisingly effective, enhancing well-being without necessitating major lifestyle overhauls.

The Power of Incremental Changes

The beauty of minor adjustments lies in their simplicity and ease of integration. Whether it's a five-minute meditation in the morning or choosing the stairs over the elevator, these acts might seem insignificant in isolation. Yet, when stitched together, they form a tapestry of improved mental and physical health that supports a more prosperous, more balanced life. This approach is not about grand gestures but about effortlessly intertwining health practices with our daily activities so that they become second nature.

Routine as a Foundation for Wellness

Establishing routines can often feel daunting; however, we sidestep the overwhelm associated with more extensive commitments by focusing on short, consistent actions. These brief activities—deep breathing during a work break or a quick post-dinner walk—can significantly boost your mood and energy levels, proving that duration is less critical than consistency. This method also allows for personalization, enabling you to tailor wellness practices to fit your unique lifestyle and needs.

Building Confidence through Self-Care

Committing to these small practices improves physical health and builds psychological resilience. Engaging regularly in self-care activities fosters a sense of accomplishment and control. Each favorable decision reinforces self-confidence and demonstrates that you have the power to influence your own life positively. Over time, these choices become ingrained habits contributing substantially to overall well-being.

Adopting such small changes requires minimal disruption yet yields measurable improvements in quality of life. This strategy makes the process less intimidating and enhances the likelihood of long-term success. By embedding simple wellness activities into our daily routines, we set the stage for sustainable health benefits supporting our mental and physical states.

Cultivating a Balanced Life

Remember, the goal here is balance—finding harmony between career ambitions and personal health without sacrificing one for the other. As we explore these themes further, we'll delve into practical ways to implement these minor adjustments and realize their profound impact on our well-being. Through real-life examples and actionable tips, we'll see how straightforward it can be to foster wellness in ways that align seamlessly with our ongoing pursuits for financial stability and personal fulfillment.

This journey is about making well-being accessible and achievable for everyone—regardless of their current lifestyle or busy schedule. Committing to these manageable steps enhances your health and enriches your overall life experience, proving that minor changes can sometimes lead to the most significant outcomes.

Small Changes, Big Rewards

Imagine your daily routine as a garden. Just as a garden thrives with regular, minor care such as watering and weeding, your well-being can bloom through small, manageable wellness practices. Integrating minor health-focused activities into your schedule doesn't require drastic changes; it's about weaving them seamlessly into your existing routine.

Small steps, like taking the stairs instead of the elevator, stretching for a few minutes every hour, or swapping a coffee for a green tea, can start to shift your health outlook without overwhelming your day. These actions are simple, yet they foster mindfulness and a proactive attitude toward health. Each step is a seed planted towards a healthier lifestyle.

Consider the impact of hydration on your energy levels and skin health. Carrying a water bottle and sipping throughout the day is a small habit, but it keeps dehydration at bay and helps maintain vital organ functions. It is a simple practice, yet its profound benefits affect everything from physical performance to cognitive function.

Minor adjustments that fit easily into most schedules include using a standing desk for part of the workday or taking a five-minute meditation break. These practices reduce the risk of chronic illnesses like obesity and type 2 diabetes, and they enhance mental health by lowering stress levels.

Small, manageable steps integrated into daily routines significantly enhance well-being, proving that simplicity often leads to success.

The Power of Incremental Change

Did you know that minor lifestyle adjustments can significantly enhance your well-being? A study by the American Psychological Association highlighted that incremental changes—like reducing sugar intake or increasing physical activity slightly—can lead to substantial health improvements over time.

Why do small changes often yield significant results? They are sustainable; they don't require vast reserves of willpower or drastic alterations to your daily life. For example, replacing one daily soda with a glass of water might seem trivial. Still, over the weeks and months, it reduces sugar intake and calorie consumption, leading to weight loss and improved insulin sensitivity.

Consider the analogy of a bank account. Just as small, regular deposits can grow into a significant sum over time, consistent small health practices can accumulate to produce notable improvements in your well-being. This approach is manageable and less daunting, making it easier to stick with long-term.

Engaging in short, daily walks, even during office breaks, can boost cardiovascular health, aid digestion, and improve mental clarity. Each step not only burns calories but also combats sedentary lifestyle risks, such as heart disease and depression.

Minor adjustments integrated into daily life can lead to profound health benefits. This incremental approach is less about making giant leaps overnight and more about consistently making better decisions.

Could recognizing the value of these minor adjustments be the key to unlocking a healthier, more vibrant you?

Committing to Daily Self-Care

Committing to routine short activities, like morning stretches or evening gratitude journaling, can boost your confidence and promote a sense of self-care. These activities don't require much time, but they send a powerful message to yourself about your worth and priority in your own life.

Small activities such as a ten-minute walk in the park, a brief meditation session, or even preparing a healthy meal can be pillars of your day's stability. Think of these activities as the brushstrokes in a larger painting—

each one might be small, but together, they create a beautiful masterpiece of health and well-being.

For many, the challenge isn't performing these activities but committing to them regularly. Setting a reminder or tying a new habit to an existing one (like meditating right after brushing your teeth) can be effective strategies for maintaining consistency.

Incorporating these practices isn't just about physical health; it's also about nurturing mental and emotional well-being. Regular self-care can reduce stress, improve mood, and increase happiness.

By weaving small, health-oriented actions into your daily routine, recognizing their profound impact on your well-being, and consistently committing to them, you set the stage for a balanced life in which health and happiness thrive together.

The simplicity of integrating small, manageable wellness practices into your daily routine can yield substantial benefits. You can significantly enhance your mental and physical well-being by committing to a few minutes of meditation, a brisk walk during your lunch break, or a short gratitude journaling session at night. These activities don't require significant shifts in your lifestyle; instead, they seamlessly blend into your existing schedule, proving that small changes can lead to substantial outcomes.

Understandably, the prospect of adding anything new to a packed day might seem daunting. However, the beauty of these minor adjustments is their feasibility. They do not demand extensive time or resources but offer a powerful return on investment regarding your health and overall happiness. By making these practices habitual, you foster an environment where well-being evolves from an occasional act to a regular, effortless part of your life.

Moreover, these small steps serve as the building blocks for greater confidence and self-care. Whenever you choose a healthy snack over junk food or take the stairs instead of the elevator, you reinforce a commitment to your health and personal growth. These choices accumulate, leading to improved physical fitness, enhanced mood, and increased energy levels—all crucial for sustaining individual and professional success.

Remember, the journey to improved well-being must not be radical or overwhelming. Start where you are, use what you have, and do what you can. Over time, these little tweaks to your daily routine will become second nature and inspire further positive changes. With each small step, you are paving the way to a more fulfilled and balanced life.

Embrace these practices with an open heart and mind. Trust in their potential to transform your life subtly but profoundly. Here's to finding balance and blooming into the best version of yourself—one small step at a time.

Reflection Questions

- **Personal Reflection:** What small change from this chapter can you start incorporating into your routine today? How do you think this will affect your overall well-being over time?
- **Consistency Challenge:** Which of the small practices mentioned (e.g., taking the stairs, meditation, and hydration) do you believe will be the easiest for you to stick with? What steps can you take to ensure consistency in practicing it daily?
- **Overcoming Resistance:** What barriers do you anticipate when trying to implement these small changes? How can you address or overcome these challenges to make the changes sustainable?
- **Health and Balance:** Reflecting on your current lifestyle, where do you see the biggest opportunity for integrating simple wellness practices? How can you balance these changes with your existing commitments?
- **Tracking Progress:** How will you measure the impact of these small changes on your life? Consider setting a simple goal or tracking a habit related to the practices in this chapter to assess your progress.

CHAPTER 10

INVESTMENT BASICS – BUILDING WEALTH ONE STEP AT A TIME

Can Modest Means Forge a Path to Wealth?

Ella stood at the kitchen counter, her fingers stained with the morning's blueberry jam, as sunlight spilled across the old oak table. She held a crumpled bank statement between her fingers, her eyes tracing over each figure as if they might morph into something more promising. The aroma of freshly brewed coffee mingled with the lingering scent of toast, creating a comforting yet stark contrast to the chill of her financial reality.

Her mind wandered to last night's conversation with her sister, Lydia, who had extolled investment virtues—even for those who believed they had little to spare. "It's not just for the wealthy," Lydia had said, her voice crackling through the phone line, infused with excitement and conviction. Ella remembered how her sister described the magic of compound interest and the accessibility of new platforms that catered even to those who could only invest small amounts.

Ella's thoughts were interrupted by the children's laughter outside as she poured herself a cup of coffee. She momentarily watched them through the window, their carefree movements stark against her heavy contemplations. They raced up and down on their bicycles under the broad maple trees whose leaves were beginning to hint at autumn's approach.

Ella sat down with her coffee and opened her laptop. The screen lit up, revealing a bookmarked article on robo-advisors—automated platforms that promised to make investing simple and tailored to one's financial capacity and risk tolerance. Her heart fluttered with hope and skepticism as she read about algorithms designed to optimize investments over time. Could such a tool bridge the gap between her financial strain and future security?

She imagined what it might be like not to wince at every unexpected expense—to not feel like every dollar was a soldier in a battle where defeat seemed certain. The thought brought both warmth and a twinge of fear; hope was a risky commodity in her world.

As Ella sipped her coffee, feeling its warmth seep through her, she pondered whether stepping into this unknown world of investment was merely another gamble or if it could genuinely be the lifeline Lydia believed it to be. Could small regular contributions accumulate into something substantial? Could these modest seeds grow into a sturdy tree under which she might one day find shelter?

Is it truly feasible for anyone to build wealth through investment regardless of their initial financial standing?

From Small Seeds Grow Mighty Trees

Investing isn't just for the affluent; it's a vital tool for anyone aiming to build a secure financial future. This chapter demystifies the seemingly complex world of investments, clarifying that you don't need a fortune to start. We'll explore how even modest, consistent contributions can compound over time into substantial sums. The goal here is straightforward: to provide you with the knowledge and tools to begin your investment journey, fostering financial and emotional well-being.

Understanding the Power of Compound Interest

One of the most compelling financial concepts you will encounter is compound interest—often called the world's eighth wonder. It's the principle where your earnings generate their earnings. Here, we'll break down this concept into simple terms to show how it works tirelessly in your favor, turning small savings into a significant nest egg over time.

Investment Options for Every Income Level

The landscape of investment opportunities is vast and can be tailored to fit any budget. Whether you're considering stocks, bonds, mutual funds, or newer platforms like robo-advisors, understanding what's available is the first step towards making informed decisions. This section will guide you through these options, helping you find those that best match your financial situation and goals.

Kickstarting Your Investment Journey

For many, starting can be the hardest part. We'll introduce practical strategies focused on simplicity and accessibility. Low-cost index funds, for example, offer a way to invest in broad market segments without needing to pick individual stocks or have large amounts of capital. These funds are not only cost-effective but also automatically diversify your investment, reducing risk and requiring less of your time to manage.

Building Your Financial Confidence

Investing should empower you, not intimidate you. By understanding basic investment principles and recognizing accessible entry points, you can confidently take control of your financial future. This empowerment is crucial not just for your wallet but also for your overall mental health and well-being.

Accessible Tools for Everyone

The advent of technology in finance has democratized access to investment tools. Platforms that once were available only to the wealthy are now accessible to nearly everyone. We'll examine how these tools can help tailor an investment plan that fits your unique financial needs and risk tolerance.

Stepping Stones to Financial Dignity

Every step on your investment journey adds a stone to the foundation of your financial dignity. By investing wisely—guided by knowledge and simple yet effective tools—you're not just saving money; you're building resilience against economic uncertainty and stress.

This chapter does more than just teach about investments—it advocates for a shift in perspective where every individual sees themselves as capable investors. By fostering this mindset shift and providing practical guidance, we aim not only at wealth accumulation but also at enhancing overall life quality through financial stability and dignity.

Through this exploration, remember: the journey of a thousand miles begins with a single step. Taking that first step toward investment might be the most critical move toward securing a prosperous and dignified future.

Investing often feels intimidating, especially for those already managing financial stress. However, understanding the basics can empower anyone to take control of their financial future. At its core, investing is simply putting your money to work for you. This means purchasing assets like stocks, bonds, or real estate with the expectation that they will generate a profit over time. It's crucial to recognize that investing is not reserved for the wealthy; instead, it is a tool that can help anyone build wealth, regardless of their starting point.

One of the most powerful concepts in investing is compound interest. This is when the money you earn on your investments generates additional earnings. Over time, this can lead to exponential growth. For example, if you invest $1,000 at an annual interest rate of 5%, you will have $1,050 after one year. But in the second year, you earn interest on the new total—$1,050—resulting in $1,102.50 by year two. The longer your money has to grow, the more pronounced this effect becomes.

Many underestimate how significant even small contributions can be when invested wisely. Starting with modest amounts—say $50 a month—can lead to substantial savings due to compound interest. If invested consistently over many years, those small amounts can add up significantly as they benefit from compounding returns. This approach not only builds wealth but also instills good financial habits.

It's also essential to understand that investing isn't a one-size-fits-all approach. Different investments come with varying levels of risk and return potential. What matters most is aligning your investment choices with your personal goals and comfort level regarding risk. This alignment ensures that you remain committed and engaged with your investment strategy.

The perception that investing requires extensive knowledge or considerable capital often holds many back from taking the first step. Today's technology offers numerous resources that simplify investing for everyone. Robo-advisors are platforms that provide automated investment services tailored to individual risk tolerance and goals without requiring deep financial expertise. Individuals can start investing and see their money grow with just a few clicks.

Understanding these foundational concepts is crucial as they form the bedrock of a successful investment strategy. The sooner one grasps how investments work and recognizes the impact of compound interest, the better positioned one will be to make informed decisions about one's financial future. Fostering a mindset where investing becomes an integral part of your financial planning rather than an intimidating hurdle is essential.

As you learn more about investments and how they can fit into your life, remember that it's never too late to start investing. Even if you feel behind or overwhelmed by past choices or missed opportunities, remember that every step forward counts toward building a more secure financial future.

Ready to Explore Diverse Investment Options?

Understanding Investment Options for Everyone

Investing is not just a privilege for the wealthy; it is a pathway available to everyone, regardless of their financial background. The first step in your investment journey is understanding the various options available. These options can cater to different income levels and financial goals. This knowledge empowers you to make informed choices that align with your aspirations.

Stocks, bonds, and mutual funds are the most common investment vehicles. Stocks represent company ownership and can yield high returns but also have higher risks. If you're new to investing or have a lower risk tolerance, you might consider starting with bonds, which are generally more stable and provide regular interest payments. Mutual funds combine money from multiple investors to purchase a diversified portfolio of stocks and bonds, making them an excellent option for those who want professional management without needing substantial capital.

Another accessible option is exchange-traded funds (ETFs). Like mutual funds, ETFs allow you to invest in a collection of assets but trade like stocks on an exchange. They often have lower fees than mutual funds and provide instant diversification even with modest investments. This means you can spread your risk across various sectors or asset classes without needing a large amount of capital upfront.

For those who may feel overwhelmed by the complexity of traditional investing, robo-advisors present a user-friendly alternative. These automated platforms assess your financial situation and goals and create an investment portfolio tailored to your needs. They typically require lower minimum investments than traditional advisors and offer diversified portfolios managed through algorithms that adjust based on market conditions and risk tolerance.

If you're looking for something even more straightforward, consider high-yield savings accounts or certificates of deposit (CDs). While these don't offer high returns like stocks or mutual funds, they provide security and guaranteed returns on your investment over time.

This approach may not make you rich overnight, but it helps build a foundation for future investments while keeping your funds accessible.

Moreover, don't overlook real estate crowdfunding as a viable option for generating passive income without purchasing entire properties yourself. Platforms exist where you can invest in real estate projects with smaller amounts of capital, allowing you to diversify into real estate without the burdens associated with direct ownership.

It's crucial to recognize that every investment comes with its own set of risks and rewards. Conducting thorough research before choosing any specific option will help you identify what aligns best with your financial goals. Additionally, setting clear objectives—saving for retirement or funding a child's education—will guide your investment decisions effectively.

As you explore these diverse options, remember that the key is starting small and remaining consistent. Even modest investments can grow over time due to the power of compound interest—a concept that rewards patience and discipline in wealth accumulation. Engaging regularly with your investments will also cultivate confidence as you become more familiar with how markets operate.

In summary, whether you're considering stocks, bonds, ETFs, or alternative investment avenues like real estate crowdfunding or robo-advisors, there are many ways to build wealth, irrespective of your current financial situation. Each step taken today lays the groundwork for a more secure financial future tomorrow.

Understanding Index Funds

Investing can feel overwhelming, especially when you're starting with limited resources. One of the simplest and most effective ways to enter the investment world is through low-cost index funds. These funds track a specific market index, such as the S&P 500, offering broad market exposure without requiring extensive research or expertise. Investing in an index fund means buying a small piece of many companies at once, making it a practical choice for anyone looking to build wealth over time.

One of the key advantages of index funds is their low fees. Traditional, actively managed funds often charge higher management fees because they rely on professionals to pick stocks. In contrast, index funds are passively managed; they aim to replicate the performance of a specific index. Lower fees mean more of your money stays invested, allowing it to grow through compound interest. Over time, these savings can significantly impact your investment returns.

Starting with index funds does not require a significant initial investment. Many platforms allow you to invest with minimal amounts, sometimes even as low as $100. This accessibility empowers individuals from all financial backgrounds to begin their investment journey. By contributing small amounts regularly, you can take advantage of dollar-cost averaging—an investment strategy that helps reduce volatility by spreading out purchases over time.

Setting Clear Goals

Before diving into investments, it's essential to set clear financial goals. Consider what you want to achieve: Are you saving for retirement, a home, or your child's education? Specific objectives can guide your investment choices and help maintain focus during market fluctuations. For example, if you're saving for retirement that is decades away, you might choose a more aggressive index fund that focuses on growth. Conversely, a more conservative fund might be appropriate if you're saving for a short-term goal, like a down payment on a house within five years.

Once you've established your goals, create a budget that includes regular contributions toward your investments. Treat these contributions like any other monthly expense; set it aside before allocating discretionary spending money. Automating your investments through direct deposits can simplify this process and ensure consistent contributions without requiring much thought.

Researching Investment Platforms

Choosing the right platform for investing in index funds is crucial. Look for brokerage firms that offer user-friendly interfaces, educational resources, and low trading fees. Many online brokerages cater specifically to beginners and provide tools that simplify the investing process. Some platforms even offer robo-advisors that automatically manage your portfolio based on risk tolerance and financial goals.

Take time to read reviews and compare different platforms before committing your money. Look for those that provide transparent information regarding fees and account minimums. A platform with no minimum investment requirement can benefit those just starting.

Staying Informed and Engaged

Investing doesn't end once you've purchased your index funds; staying informed about market trends and economic conditions is also essential. While it's important not to react impulsively to market fluctuations, understanding broader economic trends can help you make informed decisions about future contributions or adjustments to your portfolio.

Consider setting aside time each month to review your investments and assess whether they align with your goals. Use this opportunity to educate yourself about personal finance topics that interest you—whether it's reading articles or watching informative videos. This knowledge will empower you as an investor.

Cultivating Patience

Investing in index funds is not a get-rich-quick scheme; it requires patience and discipline. The market will experience ups and downs; however, historical data shows that staying invested typically yields positive returns over the long run. Avoid making hasty decisions based on short-term performance; focus on how your investments align with your long-term objectives.

Remember that even modest contributions add up over time thanks to compound interest—a powerful tool that works best when given time to grow. As you continue investing consistently, you'll likely witness growth in your portfolio and confidence as an investor.

Embracing Community Support

Building wealth through investing can sometimes feel isolating; connecting with others with similar goals can provide valuable support and encouragement. Seek local meetups or online forums where individuals discuss their experiences investing in index funds or personal finance in general.

Sharing insights and learning from other's successes and setbacks can enhance one's understanding of investing while fostering motivation during challenging times. Surrounding oneself with supportive peers who value financial education creates an empowering environment conducive to growth.

You're taking significant steps toward achieving financial dignity by implementing these strategies for starting an investment journey with low-cost index funds. Investing doesn't have to be daunting or exclusive; embracing simple yet effective methods tailored to your situation will better equip you for future financial success.

Investing isn't just for the affluent; it's a tool for everyone to build wealth and secure a financially stable future. By demystifying the basics of investments and illustrating the transformative power of compound interest, we've laid a foundation that empowers you, regardless of your income level, to start your investment journey confidently.

Thanks to technological advancements and the proliferation of user-friendly platforms, diverse investment options are more accessible than ever. From robo-advisors to low-cost index funds, these tools accommodate various risk tolerances and financial goals and make it feasible for anyone to begin investing with what they can afford.

The strategies we've explored for starting with simple, low-cost index funds serve as a practical entry point. This approach minimizes risks while offering exposure to the broader market's potential gains—perfect for those new to investing or looking to invest with minimal hassle.

Pathway to Prosperity: Your Investment Journey Starts Here

1. Assess Your Financial Situation: Understand your net worth, income sources, and expenses. This initial step is crucial as it sets the stage for informed decision-making about your investment capacity and needs.

2. Set Clear Investment Goals: Whether you aim for short-term gains or long-term wealth accumulation, defining your objectives is essential. It helps you tailor your investment choices to suit your financial goals.

3. Educate Yourself on Investment Vehicles: Knowledge is power. Familiarize yourself with different types of investments, such as stocks, bonds, mutual funds, and ETFs. Choose the ones that best match your risk tolerance and time horizon.

4. Establish an Investment Account: Opt for a platform that offers ease of use, low fees, and valuable educational resources. Getting started is simpler than ever, whether it's a brokerage account or an IRA.

5. Start with Low-Cost Index Funds or ETFs: These funds are ideal for beginners due to their diversified nature and lower risk profile. They're an excellent way to get broad market exposure without complex decision-making.

6. Implement Regular Investments: Use dollar-cost averaging by allocating a portion of your income to investments at regular intervals. This strategy reduces the impact of volatility and can enhance portfolio growth over time.

7. Monitor and Adjust Your Portfolio: Monitor your investments' performance and make adjustments as needed. This step is vital to aligning your portfolio with changing goals and market conditions.

8. Reinvest Dividends and Interest: Compounding can significantly increase your investments' growth potential. Reinvesting dividends and interest maximizes this effect.

9. Stay Informed and Patient: Regularly update yourself on financial news and continue learning about advanced investment strategies. Remember, investing is a marathon, not a sprint; patience is key to seeing substantial growth in your investments.

Following these steps establishes a robust framework for building and managing your investments. This structured approach simplifies the investment process and enhances your ability to achieve financial security and independence.

Remember, every investor started somewhere, and every small step you take now builds towards your larger financial goals. Keep learning, stay disciplined, and remain focused on your objectives. Your journey towards financial dignity is well within reach, powered by informed decisions and strategic investments.

Reflection Questions

- **Assessing Your Investment Readiness:** Reflect on your current financial situation. Are there small amounts you could begin contributing to an investment account? What emotions come up when you think about starting your investment journey? How can you manage any fears or uncertainties to take that first step?

- **Understanding Compound Interest:** How might the principle of compound interest impact your long-term financial goals? Can you identify a current savings goal where compounding could play a role in reaching your target? What small, consistent contributions could you make toward this goal?

- **Investment Options for Your Needs:** Based on the investment options presented (stocks, bonds, ETFs, robo-advisors, index funds, etc.), which would be most suited to your current financial situation and risk tolerance? What type of investment resonates with you the most, and why?

- **Setting Clear Financial Goals:** What are your top financial goals? Whether it's saving for retirement, a major purchase, or building an emergency fund, how can you align your investments to these goals? How will you track your progress and stay motivated?

- **Finding the Right Investment Platform:** Research and compare a few investment platforms that cater to small investors. What features are most important to you (e.g., low fees, ease of use, educational tools)? How will you decide which platform to use for your first investment?

CHAPTER 11

LIFELONG LEARNER – CONTINUOUSLY ENHANCING YOUR FINANCIAL ACUMEN

How Does One Navigate the Waters of Financial Uncertainty?

It was an overcast afternoon in the small coastal town of Seabrook. The air was thick with the salty tang of the sea, mingling with the earthy aroma of wet sand. Jonathan sat at a weathered wooden table outside a quaint café, his gaze occasionally drifting to the waves that lapped gently at the shore. His mind, however, wrestled with currents far more turbulent than those that stirred the Atlantic.

For years, Jonathan had managed his finances with casual indifference. Money came and went like the tide—sometimes high, often low, but always in motion. Yet recently, as his daughter neared college age and his retirement loomed like a distant lighthouse on a foggy night, each dollar seemed to weigh more heavily against his peace.

In his hands lay a crumpled newspaper article about continuous education in finance—a concept he had ignored as thoroughly as his old college textbooks. The words on the page spoke of empowerment and perspective shifts; money could be a source of stress and a tool for achieving goals.

Jonathan sipped his bitter and pungent coffee and recalled last week's meeting with his financial advisor. She had advised sternly yet caringly, "You need to start thinking about your financial future more seriously." He remembered how her office was filled with books on economics and finance, with podcasts playing softly in the background and discussing market trends.

Across from him sat an elderly gentleman reading something on his tablet, nodding occasionally as if agreeing with some invisible conversant. Jonathan wondered if he, too, was seeking guidance through this digital oracle or merely passing the time.

A seagull cried sharply overhead, pulling Jonathan from his reverie. He watched it soar effortlessly above the cafe, its wings slicing through the cool air. He envied its freedom—unfettered by concerns of nest eggs or tuition fees.

Placing down his cup with resolve stirring within him like spring after winter's thaw, he made up his mind to enroll in an online course on personal finance management that evening. Perhaps understanding could illuminate paths previously shadowed by ignorance.

As Jonathan folded the newspaper under his arm and prepared to leave behind the comforting sounds of clinking dishes and murmured conversations for home's quiet solitude where decisions awaited him like unopened letters, one question lingered:

Could knowledge truly dispel fear and transform money from foe to ally?

Unlock Your Financial Potential: Why Lifelong Learning is Your Greatest Asset

In a world where financial landscapes are continually evolving, the need for ongoing education in personal finance cannot be overstressed. This chapter delves into the profound impact that continual learning has on financial decision-making and overall well-being. By embracing a lifestyle of perpetual financial education, you not only enhance your understanding but also transform your relationship with money, turning it from a source of anxiety into a tool for realizing your dreams.

The Blueprint for Continuous Financial Education

The journey toward financial dignity involves more than occasional check-ins with your budget or sporadic reads of economic news. It requires a structured, consistent approach to learning. Here, we explore how to design an effective and sustainable financial education plan that fits into your life seamlessly. Whether through books that challenge your economic assumptions, podcasts that offer fresh perspectives, or online courses that build advanced skills, each resource plays a pivotal role in crafting a well-rounded financial intellect.

Keeping Pace with the Ever-Changing Financial Trends

The financial world is dynamic, with new trends and technologies reshaping how we think about and manage money. Staying updated isn't just about keeping abreast of the latest news; it's about understanding how these changes affect you personally and professionally. This chapter will highlight why keeping your finger on the pulse of financial trends is crucial and how it empowers you to make informed decisions that align with your long-term goals.

Transforming Your Money Mindset

Knowledge is power, especially when it comes to finances. Each new piece of information has the potential to shift how you view and handle money. This section will discuss how enhanced knowledge and continuous learning can change your perspective from seeing money as a perennial source of stress to viewing it as a valuable resource that supports your aspirations. Changing your mindset will pave the way for more confident and assertive financial decisions.

Through these focal points, this chapter aims to equip you with the tools and insights necessary to navigate your financial journey with greater ease and confidence. Emphasizing practical steps and real-life applications, we strive to transform theoretical knowledge into tangible actions that enhance economic stability and mental peace.

Remember, financial dignity is not achieved overnight or by chance—it's cultivated through disciplined learning and thoughtful application of knowledge. Let's embark on this educational journey together, ensuring that each step taken is one step closer to mastering the art of personal finance in a way that respects and enhances your life's quality.

Fostering an environment where continuous learning is valued safeguards your financial future and contributes to a legacy of wisdom and stability that can be passed down through generations. Let's turn the page on economic uncertainty and start writing a story of empowerment, security, and enduring prosperity.

Designing a financial education plan is crucial to gaining control over your financial situation. This plan is a roadmap, guiding you through the myriad resources available today. With the right approach, you can transform your financial knowledge from overwhelming to empowering. Start by identifying your current level of understanding and your specific goals. This self-assessment will help you tailor your learning journey, ensuring that you focus on areas that matter most to you.

Books are often the first resource people think of when embarking on an educational journey. They provide in-depth knowledge and can cover various topics, from budgeting to investing. Consider setting a goal to read at least one personal finance book each month. Look for highly recommended titles or bestsellers that resonate with your current challenges or aspirations. Creating a reading list and sticking to it can keep you motivated and accountable.

Podcasts have surged in popularity due to their accessibility and engaging formats. You can listen while commuting, exercising, or cooking—making incorporating financial learning into your daily routine effortless. Look for podcasts that feature expert interviews, real-life stories, and practical advice. Aim for a mix of content that covers both foundational concepts and advanced strategies. This variety will help deepen your understanding while keeping the content fresh and interesting.

Online courses are another valuable resource for enhancing your financial acumen. Websites like Coursera, Udemy, or Khan Academy offer structured courses on diverse topics such as investing, tax planning, and retirement savings. Many courses are free or cheap, making them accessible regardless of budget. Set aside time each week to complete lessons and engage with course materials actively; this will reinforce what you've learned and allow for deeper comprehension.

Incorporating financial news sources into your education plan is essential for staying current with market trends and economic changes. Subscribing to reputable financial news outlets or newsletters can provide insights into what's happening in finance. Make it a habit to read articles regularly or set alerts for topics relevant to your interests—this practice keeps you informed. It helps you connect theoretical knowledge with real-world applications.

Networking with others who are also focused on improving their financial literacy can be incredibly beneficial. Join online forums, local meetups, or social media groups dedicated to personal finance discussions. Engaging in these communities allows you to share experiences, ask questions, and learn from others' successes and setbacks. Building relationships with like-minded individuals provides support and motivation as you navigate this path together.

Creating an ongoing education plan requires commitment and consistency. Schedule regular check-ins with yourself to assess progress in your learning journey. Are there areas where you're struggling? Are there new resources you'd like to explore? Adjusting your plan as needed ensures it remains relevant and effective in meeting your evolving needs.

By establishing a structured approach to continuous learning about finance, you're taking significant steps toward achieving greater confidence in managing money. This proactive stance not only enhances your knowledge but also transforms how you perceive financial challenges—from sources of anxiety into opportunities for growth.

Ready to Explore the Importance of Staying Updated With Financial Trends?

The Need for Continuous Financial Awareness

Staying updated with financial trends and strategies is crucial in today's fast-paced world. Markets change, regulations evolve, and new investment opportunities arise. Without a solid grasp of these developments, making informed financial decisions becomes increasingly challenging. This ongoing education enhances your economic understanding and equips you with the confidence to navigate complex choices effectively.

Regular engagement with financial content is vital.

Subscribing to reputable financial news sources, reading articles, or following influential finance personalities on social media can inform you about market movements and economic shifts. Podcasts are also an excellent resource, offering insights from experts that you can absorb during your daily commute or while exercising. These habits transform passive consumption into active learning.

Courses provide structured knowledge that can significantly enhance your understanding of finance.

Many platforms offer free or low-cost classes ranging from personal finance to advanced investing strategies. By dedicating time each month to complete a course, you can build a robust foundation that empowers better decision-making. Choose subjects that resonate with your goals; whether it's budgeting basics or stock market strategies, there's something for everyone.

Understanding the context behind current events is equally important. Economic indicators like inflation rates or employment statistics directly affect personal finance. For example, if inflation rises, your money's purchasing power decreases. Staying informed allows you to adjust your financial strategies accordingly, whether that means reassessing your budget or exploring alternative investments.

Networking within finance-focused communities can also be beneficial.

Engaging with similar interests offers the opportunity to exchange ideas and experiences. Joining online forums or local investment clubs enables you to learn from diverse perspectives while building a support system. This communal learning often leads to discovering resources or strategies that may not be on your radar.

As technology evolves, new tools and apps emerge that simplify managing finances. Embracing these innovations can streamline budgeting and investing efforts while keeping you attuned to changing market dynamics. Consider using budgeting apps that track spending patterns or investment platforms that provide real-time market insights—these tools can enhance your financial literacy and help you make timely decisions.

Recognizing the emotional aspect of money management is equally essential. Financial stress often stems from uncertainty and lack of knowledge. By committing to continuous education, you shift from feeling overwhelmed by finances to feeling empowered by them. This transformation creates a healthier mindset around money, allowing you to see it as a tool for achieving goals rather than a source of anxiety.

Finally, remember that learning is a lifelong journey. The financial landscape will constantly evolve, presenting new challenges and opportunities. By prioritizing continuous education, you're not just enhancing your skills but investing in your future security and well-being. Each step toward expanding your knowledge contributes to building a more confident approach to managing finances—a critical aspect of reclaiming control over your financial life.

Shifting Your Mindset about Money

Many people view money primarily as a source of stress. This perspective can be overwhelming and limiting, often leading to feelings of inadequacy or anxiety. However, transforming your understanding of money can significantly improve your financial well-being. When you see money as a tool for achieving your goals rather than just a necessity, you empower yourself to make better decisions.

To facilitate this shift in perspective, begin by educating yourself about financial concepts. Familiarizing yourself with budgeting, saving, investing, and debt management provides a solid foundation. Start with resources that resonate with you; find materials that spark your interest, whether it's engaging podcasts, informative books, or interactive online courses. The goal is to build confidence in your financial knowledge and skills.

Setting clear financial goals is an effective strategy for reframing how you think about money. Consider what you want to achieve financially— buying a home, starting a business, or planning retirement. Write down these goals and break them into smaller, actionable steps. This approach makes the process feel more manageable and shifts your focus from scarcity to abundance.

Engaging with financial communities can further enhance this transformation. Surround yourself with individuals who share similar aspirations or challenges. Online forums, local meetups, or social media groups can offer support and accountability while providing fresh insights and diverse perspectives on financial management. Sharing experiences fosters a sense of belonging and encourages positive discussions around money.

Practicing gratitude for what you currently have can also reshape your relationship with money. Instead of fixating on what you lack or what's causing stress, acknowledge the resources at your disposal—be it skills, income, or supportive relationships. This mindset shift cultivates appreciation and reduces feelings of deprivation.

As you gain knowledge and set goals, remember that mistakes are part of learning. Everyone encounters setbacks; it's how you respond that matters most. Approach these moments with compassion for yourself and an understanding that growth often comes from overcoming challenges. Reflect on what went wrong and use those lessons to inform future decisions.

Investing time in self-reflection is crucial in transforming your financial perspective. Regularly assess your beliefs about money and identify any negative thought patterns that may arise. Challenge these thoughts by replacing them with positive affirmations focused on abundance and opportunity.

Ultimately, enhancing your financial acumen equips you to make informed decisions confidently. With each step taken towards more excellent knowledge and understanding, you'll notice a change in your finances and how you perceive yourself in relation to money—a shift from anxiety to empowerment where choices become opportunities rather than burdens.

Embarking on a journey of continuous financial learning is not just about enhancing your knowledge; it's about transforming your relationship with money. By designing an ongoing education plan, staying updated with the latest financial trends, and reshaping your money management perspectives, you equip yourself with the tools necessary for making empowered and informed decisions.

Continuous education is vital. It fortifies your decision-making abilities, helping you confidently navigate the complexities of finance. This process involves regular engagement with books, podcasts, and online courses, which are readily accessible and can be tailored to fit your learning style and schedule. Remember, every knowledge acquired is a step toward greater financial security.

Understanding current financial trends and strategies is equally crucial. The economic landscape is ever-evolving, influenced by global events, technological advancements, and new regulatory policies. By keeping yourself informed, you safeguard your assets and spot opportunities that others might overlook. This proactive approach is essential in maintaining and growing your financial resources effectively.

Perhaps the most profound benefit of lifelong learning in finance is transforming your perspective on money management. Knowledge empowers you to see money not as a source of stress but as a valuable tool for achieving your dreams. This shift in perspective opens up new possibilities for budgeting, investing, and saving, ensuring that financial decisions support your long-term well-being and happiness.

Through these steps, you are not just planning for your financial future; you are actively shaping it. Each strategy you learn and apply contributes to a foundation of financial dignity—decisions are driven by knowledge and confidence rather than fear or uncertainty.

By fostering a habit of continuous learning, you also set a powerful example for others around you—be it family, friends, or colleagues. Your journey can inspire them to embark on their paths toward financial enlightenment and security.

In essence, lifelong learning in finance is about creating a sustainable and fulfilling relationship with money. It's about taking control, making informed choices, and moving confidently toward your financial goals. Let this journey be one of empowerment, growth, and personal fulfillment. Remember, the path to financial dignity is paved with knowledge, and every step you take enriches your bank account and your life.

Reflection Questions

- What steps have you taken recently to improve your understanding of personal finance?
  Reflect on any specific resources, courses, or habits you've adopted to expand your financial knowledge.
- How do you currently view money—as a source of stress, a tool for achieving goals, or something else?
  Consider how this perspective has shaped your financial decisions and explore ways to transform your mindset.
- What actions can you take today to stay updated with financial trends and developments?
  Identify reliable sources like books, podcasts, or financial news outlets to integrate into your daily routine.
- What is one financial goal you want to achieve in the next year, and how can continuous learning help you reach it?
  Reflect on the skills or knowledge you need to acquire to accomplish this goal.
- How can you engage with a community of like-minded individuals to enhance your financial literacy?
  Explore forums, local groups, or online communities that align with your financial goals and interests.

Summary of Actions to Implement

- Create a Financial Education Plan
  List specific resources (e.g., books, podcasts, courses) to study over the next few months.
- Set Regular Learning Goals
  Commit to mastering one financial topic per month, such as budgeting, investing, or retirement planning.
- Stay Updated
  Subscribe to financial newsletters or set alerts for market trends and news relevant to your goals.
- Engage with Financial Communities
  Join groups or forums where you can share experiences and learn from others.
- Utilize Financial Tools
  Experiment with budgeting apps or investment platforms to streamline your financial management.
- Reassess and Adjust
  Schedule quarterly check-ins to evaluate progress, refine your learning plan, and explore new resources.

CHAPTER 12

CONSULTING THE PROS – WHEN TO SEEK FINANCIAL ADVICE

When Does Seeking Guidance Become Necessary?

The morning light filtered through the blinds, casting long shadows across the living room where Michael sat, enveloped in a sea of paperwork and digital screens. His brow was furrowed, and his eyes scanned numbers that danced too quickly from one category to another. Investments, mortgages, college funds for his twins—the figures swirled in his mind like leaves caught in an autumn breeze.

Outside, the world hummed with the ordinary: cars whispered along the nearby street, and a dog enthusiastically barked at a squirrel daring enough to invade its garden. But inside, Michael's world was anything but ordinary as he contemplated the complexities of his financial decisions. The weight of ensuring a stable future for his family pressed cold and hard against his chest.

He vividly remembered the days when such matters seemed simpler. A younger Michael had believed that hard work alone would suffice, that savings would naturally grow like trees steadily reaching the sky. But time had taught him differently. Markets could shift like sand underfoot without warning, and what once seemed solid could suddenly slip away.

His wife Laura walked in quietly, her presence a calming breeze. She glanced at the screen, then at Michael's clenched jaw. "Maybe it's time we get some help," she suggested gently, placing a warm hand on his shoulder.

Michael looked up into her reassuring eyes and considered it—professional advice might indeed be what they needed to navigate this stormy sea of numbers and forecasts. The thought brought relief and reluctance; admitting he needed help felt like admitting defeat.

Yet, as he watched a leaf break free from its branch outside the window, twirling gracefully before settling on the ground, he realized there was wisdom in knowing when to hold on and let go.

Could seeking professional financial advice offer them guidance and peace of mind?

Unlocking the Door to Financial Clarity and Freedom

Navigating the complexities of personal finance can often feel like trying to find your way through a labyrinth without a map. This is precisely where professional financial advice can serve as your compass, guiding you toward more apparent, strategic decision-making. The journey towards financial dignity involves understanding when and why to seek out this guidance and recognizing the comprehensive benefits it brings—not just for managing wealth but for fostering peace of mind.

Recognizing When It's Time to Consult a Professional

There are pivotal moments in life when consulting with a financial advisor becomes helpful and essential. Whether you're facing major life transitions such as marriage, the birth of a child, significant career changes, or planning for retirement, these events can drastically alter your financial landscape. In these times, the expertise of a financial advisor can be invaluable in helping you reassess your plans and ensure they fit your evolving needs.

Moreover, suppose you are overwhelmed by the options available or confused about managing your assets effectively. In that case, this signals that professional guidance could alleviate stress and provide clarity. For many, managing finances alone can lead to missed opportunities or costly mistakes; thus, recognizing this need is the first step towards regaining control and confidence in your financial decisions.

Choosing the Right Financial Advisor

Selecting someone to trust with your financial future is no small decision. In this chapter, we will explore how to identify advisors who are qualified and who resonate with your personal goals and values. It's essential to look for credentials and a solid track record, but equally vital is finding someone who listens—to understand your unique situation—ensuring their advice aligns with your long-term objectives.

The Holistic Approach to Financial Planning

Beyond mere numbers and data analysis, experienced advisors bring a holistic perspective to wealth management. They consider all facets of your life—your family structure, career aspirations, health considerations, and even your fears and hopes. This comprehensive approach ensures that all recommendations are tailored specifically to support your financial health and overall well-being.

The real value lies in crafting strategies that grow with you over time, adjusting as your life unfolds and new goals come into focus. Holistic planning means looking beyond immediate concerns to secure your future financially while building resilience against unexpected challenges.

Empowering Your Financial Journey

This chapter aims to inform and empower you with the knowledge needed to make informed decisions about when and how to seek financial advice. With expert insights, you'll be better equipped to navigate the sometimes turbulent waters of personal finance. This guidance is not just about improving numbers on a spreadsheet; it's about enhancing the quality of life.

By demystifying the process of engaging with financial professionals and highlighting the profound impact they can have on an individual's fiscal health, we strive to provide you with the tools and confidence necessary for achieving true financial dignity. Remember: seeking help isn't a sign of weakness—it's an astute strategy for anyone serious about building a secure and prosperous future.

When managing finances, recognizing when to seek professional advice can significantly influence your financial well-being. Many people find themselves in complex situations requiring more than basic budgeting skills. Understanding the right moments to consult a financial advisor can improve decision-making and enhance financial health.

For instance, if you're facing a significant life change, such as getting married, having a child, or changing careers, this could be an ideal time to seek expert guidance. These transitions often come with new financial responsibilities and decisions that may feel overwhelming. A financial advisor can help you navigate the intricacies of these changes, providing tailored advice on budgeting for new expenses or planning for long-term goals like education savings or retirement.

Another scenario where professional advice proves invaluable is during periods of economic uncertainty. If you're worried about job security or market volatility impacting your investments, speaking with an advisor can help you assess your risk tolerance and develop a plan to protect your assets. They can offer strategies that align with your financial goals while accounting for current market conditions, thus alleviating some of the stress from navigating unpredictable environments.

If you're struggling with debt management, consulting a financial professional is wise. Whether you have student loans, credit card debt, or medical bills, an advisor can work with you to create a structured repayment plan tailored to your situation. They can also provide insights into consolidation options or strategies to improve your credit score, helping you regain control over your finances.

Additionally, individuals nearing retirement often benefit from consulting experts who specialize in retirement planning. As retirement approaches, the need for strategic withdrawal plans and understanding Social Security benefits becomes paramount. An advisor can assist in optimizing these areas, ensuring a sustainable income that lasts throughout retirement.

For those looking to invest but feeling overwhelmed by the array of choices and strategies, seeking professional advice is essential. The investment landscape offers a wide range of options, which can be confusing even for experienced investors. A financial advisor can provide clarity by identifying investment vehicles that align with your risk profile and goals while also helping you build a diversified portfolio designed for long-term growth.

Lastly, consulting an advisor can provide clarity and direction if you feel that your financial knowledge is lacking or if you've experienced significant life events—such as divorce or inheritance. These situations often carry emotional weight and complex financial implications. Professional guidance can help you make informed decisions rather than reactive ones driven by stress or confusion.

Recognizing these scenarios where professional guidance could enhance financial management is essential for creating a stable future. Taking proactive steps now will pave the way for informed decision-making and empower you toward achieving greater financial dignity.

What's Next: Finding the Right Financial Advisor?

Understanding Your Needs

Choosing the right financial advisor begins with clearly understanding your financial situation and goals. Take time to reflect on what you hope to achieve. Are you seeking help with budgeting, retirement planning, or investment strategies? Each of these areas requires different expertise, so knowing where you need support is essential. Identifying your specific needs will guide you in selecting an advisor specializing in those areas.

Researching Credentials

Once you have a clear picture of your financial objectives, start researching potential advisors. Look for professionals with recognized credentials. Designations such as Certified Financial Planner (CFP), Chartered Financial Analyst (CFA), or Personal Financial Specialist (PFS) indicate a level of expertise and commitment to ethical standards. Don't hesitate to ask for proof of their qualifications; this step is crucial in ensuring you're working with someone with the necessary knowledge and skills.

Evaluating Experience

Experience matters when it comes to financial advising. Seek out advisors who have worked with clients in similar situations to yours. For instance, if you're a young professional starting your career, find someone who understands the challenges and opportunities of that phase of life. Inquire about their track record—successful case studies can provide insight into how they approach various financial issues and whether they can effectively address your concerns.

Assessing Communication Style

Communicating complex financial concepts is vital in a successful advisor-client relationship. Please consider how potential advisors explain their services and strategies during initial consultations. Do they listen actively to your concerns? Are they patient in answering questions? A good advisor should be able to break down intricate topics into simple terms, making sure you're comfortable with the information provided. This rapport is essential for a productive working relationship.

Understanding Fee Structures

Financial advisors operate under different fee structures, which can significantly impact your overall costs. Some charge a flat fee, while others may take a percentage of assets managed or earn commissions on products sold. Understanding how an advisor gets paid is important because this can influence their recommendations. Be sure to ask about any hidden fees or additional charges that may arise during the advisory relationship.

Seeking Recommendations

Word-of-mouth referrals can be one of the most reliable ways to find a trustworthy advisor. Reach out to friends, family members, or colleagues who have had positive experiences with financial professionals. Personal recommendations often provide insights beyond what online reviews may show, helping you feel more confident in your choice.

Conducting Interviews

After narrowing down your list of potential advisors, schedule interviews with them. This is an opportunity for them to assess your situation and for you to evaluate their fit for your needs. Prepare questions addressing your concerns and gauge their responses regarding investment philosophies, risk management strategies, and client communication practices. This dialogue will help clarify whether they align with your values and financial goals.

Trust Your instincts

Finally, trust your instincts when choosing an advisor. Even if someone has impressive credentials and experience, it's crucial that you feel comfortable discussing sensitive financial matters with them. Your relationship should be built on trust and mutual respect; if something feels off during your interactions, don't hesitate to keep looking until you find someone who feels right.

By carefully considering these factors when choosing a financial advisor, you'll position yourself for success on your path to achieving financial dignity and peace of mind through effective financial management.

Comprehensive Financial Insights

Seeking professional financial advice offers numerous benefits that extend beyond mere investment strategies. Experienced advisors provide a holistic approach to financial planning, which means they consider all aspects of an individual's economic life. This includes income, expenses, savings, investments, insurance, and estate planning. Viewing the whole picture can help clients create a more cohesive and effective financial strategy that aligns with their goals and values.

One significant advantage of working with a professional is the ability to clarify complex situations. Financial matters can often feel overwhelming due to jargon and intricate details. An advisor can break down these complexities into understandable terms. For instance, if you're grappling with debt management or retirement planning, an advisor can outline clear steps and help you prioritize actions based on your circumstances.

Additionally, a holistic financial plan considers not just immediate goals but also long-term aspirations. Advisors often utilize tools like cash flow analysis and risk assessment to develop strategies tailored to your needs. They will ask about your short-term objectives—like buying a home or funding education—and long-term dreams, such as retirement or leaving a legacy. This forward-thinking approach ensures that every decision made today supports your future.

Emotional Support and Accountability

Navigating finances can be emotionally taxing. Many individuals experience anxiety around money, which may lead to poor decision-making. A financial advisor acts as an educator and a supportive partner in this journey. They reassure during turbulent times and help keep emotions in check when making critical decisions. Having someone who understands the emotional weight of financial choices can significantly alleviate stress.

Moreover, professional guidance fosters accountability. When you work with an advisor, you establish a relationship built on trust where you can openly discuss your financial habits and behaviors. This accountability encourages better spending and saving practices while reinforcing the commitment to achieving your goals. Knowing someone is monitoring your progress can be highly motivating.

Customized Strategies for Diverse Needs

Every individual's financial situation is unique and influenced by age, income level, family dynamics, and personal values. Experienced advisors tailor their strategies accordingly. For example, young professionals may focus on student loan repayment and building credit, while those nearing retirement might prioritize investment growth and withdrawal strategies.

Advisors also recognize that life events—such as marriage, divorce, or career changes—can significantly impact financial plans. They are equipped to adjust strategies as circumstances evolve, ensuring your plan remains relevant and effective over time.

Navigating Regulatory Changes

The financial landscape is constantly changing due to regulations and market conditions. Keeping abreast of these shifts requires expertise that many individuals don't have the time or resources to maintain. A seasoned advisor stays informed about new laws that could affect taxes or investment opportunities, allowing them to offer proactive advice that protects your interests.

This vigilance helps clients avoid potential pitfalls associated with regulatory changes while maximizing advantages related to tax breaks or incentives available at different life stages.

Wealth Building through Strategic Planning

Holistic financial planning emphasizes wealth building through informed decision-making rather than speculative risks. Advisors guide clients in identifying suitable investment vehicles based on their risk tolerance and time horizon. Instead of chasing trends or reacting impulsively to market fluctuations, clients gradually learn how to build wealth through disciplined investing aligned with their overall plan.

This approach also fosters financial literacy, empowering clients to make informed choices independently.

Conclusion: A Collaborative Journey

Ultimately, engaging with a professional for holistic financial planning is not merely about managing money; it's about fostering a collaborative relationship to achieve peace of mind regarding one's finances. The benefits are multifaceted, from clarity in understanding complex issues to personalized strategies that adapt as life evolves.

By prioritizing this partnership with an experienced advisor, individuals can unlock more significant potential for achieving their dreams while alleviating the burdens often associated with managing finances alone. As the journey progresses toward financial dignity, remember that seeking help is a step toward empowerment rather than reliance.

Navigating the financial landscape can often feel overwhelming, fraught with complexities and many choices. In these moments, seeking professional financial advice makes sense and can serve as a crucial pivot toward achieving long-term stability and peace of mind. Engaging with the right financial advisor opens the door to expert guidance tailored to your unique circumstances, helping you demystify complex scenarios and accelerate your journey toward your financial goals.

Recognizing when to seek professional advice is fundamental. Whether you're facing a significant life transition, retirement planning, or simply optimizing your investments, a financial advisor can provide invaluable insights. The benefit lies in their knowledge of markets and investment opportunities and their ability to offer holistic financial planning that encompasses all aspects of your financial life. This comprehensive approach ensures that every decision contributes positively to your financial health.

Choosing the right advisor is equally critical. It's about finding someone who has the credentials and experience and aligns with your values and financial goals. This relationship is pivotal, as the right advisor will partner in your financial journey, offering clarity and confidence in your decisions. They should empower you with knowledge and strategies, making complex financial concepts accessible and manageable.

Moreover, the holistic planning that experienced advisors offer cannot be understated. This isn't merely about picking stocks or managing assets; it's about integrating all facets of your financial life to create a cohesive strategy that supports your long-term objectives. From tax planning to estate management and insurance needs, holistic advice ensures no stone is left unturned in safeguarding and growing your wealth.

Embrace finding and working with a financial advisor as an empowering step towards greater financial clarity and security. This proactive approach alleviates stress and enhances your capability to make informed, strategic decisions that align with your immediate needs and future aspirations. Remember, seeking financial advice aims not just to improve your current financial situation but to secure a prosperous and worry-free future.

Let this understanding guide you in moving forward: professional financial advice is an investment in your future, one that bears fruit not just financially but also in the quality of life and peace of mind it brings. Equip yourself with the right support and watch as you transform challenges into stepping stones towards your financial dignity.

Reflection Questions

- **Self-Assessment of Needs**: What are the most pressing financial decisions or challenges you currently face? How confident are you in addressing them on your own?
- **Recognizing the Right Moment**: Reflect on a time when financial advice could have improved your outcomes. What signs would you look for now to recognize the need for professional guidance?
- **Evaluating Holistic Benefits**: How might having a financial advisor provide you with not only better financial management but also peace of mind?
- **Choosing the Right Fit**: What qualities would you prioritize when selecting a financial advisor? How would you ensure their values and strategies align with your personal and financial goals?
- **Taking Proactive Steps**: What specific actions will you take this month to research financial advisors or explore if professional guidance could enhance your financial planning?

Summary of Actions to Implement:

- Identify and list your top financial goals and challenges.
- Research at least three financial advisors with reputable credentials (e.g., CFP, CFA) and assess their experience and client reviews.
- Schedule consultations to evaluate how they address your unique needs and communicate complex topics.
- Discuss and confirm fee structures to ensure transparency.
- Begin implementing the initial strategies provided by your chosen advisor and review progress regularly.

CHAPTER 13

NO AGE LIMIT – STARTING YOUR FINANCIAL PLAN TODAY

Can Financial Planning Start Too Late?

In the quiet suburb of Maplewood, under the soft glow of a late afternoon sun, Thomas shuffled papers across his kitchen table. They rustled like dry leaves in autumn, each sheet a testament to years spent avoiding this task. At 45, Thomas had spent his life chasing dreams that danced just beyond his reach—opening a café that never turned a profit, investing in stocks that promised much but yielded little. Now, surrounded by bills and bank statements, he wondered if the clock had ticked too far past hope.

The coffee pot gurgled in the background, filling the room with the rich scent of dark roast. He poured himself a cup, the steam warming his face as he pondered over an article he had stumbled upon online. It spoke of financial planning as a timeless endeavor, not confined to the eager hands of youth but open to all who dared to grasp it. The concept was simple yet profound: it was never too late to start organizing one's finances.

Outside, children's laughter floated through the open window, mingling with the chirping of early evening crickets. The sounds pulled him momentarily from his reverie; how swiftly those young voices would grow into adulthood, facing their fiscal realities. He sipped his coffee and allowed himself a moment's envy for their ignorance of time's relentless march.

Returning to his financial assessment, Thomas considered his modest savings account—a small pool gathered from years of cautious labor—and the modest pension that lay in wait. Could these be marshaled into something more? The article suggested steps: assess current assets and liabilities, set realistic goals, create a budget, and consider long-term investments even at this stage.

As he mapped out potential plans on paper—scribbling figures, erasing doubts—he felt an unfamiliar stir: hope mingled with resolve. Perhaps starting now wasn't just possible; maybe it was precisely what he needed. His thoughts were interrupted by the low hum of the refrigerator kicking on and off—a reminder of all things persistent and enduring.

Could others like Thomas find solace and direction in taking control of their financial destiny later in life?

Is It Ever Too Late to Start Planning Your Finances?

Imagine you're at a stage in your life where the days of youth seem like a distant echo and the responsibilities of adulthood fully anchor your daily reality. It's easy to fall into the trap of thinking that the best time to start financial planning has slipped unnoticed during your younger years. However, this chapter is dedicated to dismantling that myth and proving that when it comes to securing your financial future, the best time is now—regardless of whether you're in your 30s, 40s, or beyond.

Dispelling Age-Related Myths

The first step towards embracing financial planning at any age is to let go of deep-seated myths. Many believe that effective financial planning is reserved for the young or that middle age is too late to make meaningful changes. Here, we'll dismantle these misconceptions and show how starting later can still lead to substantial achievements. Our goal is to challenge these notions and replace them with a practical understanding that every day presents a new opportunity to improve your financial health.

Tailored Strategies for New Beginnings

For those who think they've missed the mark, remember that each chapter in life offers unique opportunities and challenges. This section will introduce effective financial strategies specifically designed for middle-aged people starting their journey. By focusing on tailored advice, we aim to provide actionable steps that can be implemented immediately, regardless of your starting point.

Empowering Financial Confidence

Lastly, developing confidence is crucial in managing your finances effectively. It's one thing to know what needs to be done and another to feel empowered enough to do it. Here, we will explore how taking control of your finances can lead to economic stability and a more profound sense of personal achievement and security. We'll encourage you by sharing stories of individuals who have triumphed over their late starts and showing you that perseverance and informed decision-making can yield transformative results.

At its core, this chapter seeks not just to inform but also to inspire. By confronting and overcoming the intimidation often associated with late-start financial planning, you can unlock the potential that aligns with personal and economic growth. Whether you are just starting or looking for a way back on track, the strategies discussed here are designed with one purpose: to empower you.

We understand that embarking on this journey might seem daunting initially—especially if you're comparing yourself against societal benchmarks or younger counterparts—but part of our discussion will focus on fostering an environment where each step forward is celebrated as a victory.

By the end of this chapter, our aim is for you to have gained not only knowledge but also confidence—a confidence rooted not in the years gone by but in the possibilities ahead. The practical steps outlined here are intended as tools for liberation from financial stress and anxiety, paving the way toward financial dignity and holistic well-being.

So, let's begin this journey together, embracing each challenge as an opportunity for growth and each success as a stepping stone toward achieving lasting financial peace and dignity.

Financial planning often seems reserved for the young, successful professionals who appear to have their lives together. This stereotype can create a significant barrier, leading many individuals in their 30s or 40s to believe they have missed the boat on financial planning. However, this notion is misleading. Financial planning is not an age-specific activity; it's a lifelong necessity. The reality is that starting your financial journey at any age can lead to empowerment and peace of mind.

Many people think they should have everything figured out by their 20s. This belief can foster feelings of inadequacy and despair in those just beginning to confront their finances later in life. The truth is that financial literacy doesn't come with age; it develops through experience and intention. If you find yourself in your 30s or 40s, it's essential to recognize that you're not alone or behind schedule. Countless individuals begin their financial journeys later and achieve remarkable success.

There is a common misconception that one must possess substantial savings or investments before considering financial planning. This can deter many from seeking help or guidance. In reality, anyone can start where they are—with whatever available resources. Whether managing debt, saving for retirement, or starting a new investment strategy, taking small steps today can lead to significant changes over time.

Another myth is that financial planning is only for those nearing retirement age. This assumption neglects the critical importance of setting goals earlier on. Planning allows you to align your financial strategies with your life aspirations, whether buying a home, funding education for children or traveling the world. The earlier you start thinking about these goals, the more options you will have when it comes time to make them a reality.

Moreover, some believe that it's too late to catch up if they haven't started investing by a certain age. This fear often paralyzes individuals into inaction. The power of compound interest means even late starters can build wealth over time; every contribution counts! By starting now, regardless of prior experience or savings level, individuals can leverage the time they have left to grow their assets strategically.

It's also important to highlight that financial planning should not be viewed as an overwhelming task meant only for experts. Instead, it should be seen as an ongoing process involving setting realistic goals and regularly revisiting them. You don't need a finance degree to create a solid plan; there are numerous resources available—books, online courses, workshops—that cater specifically to beginners at any age.

In essence, letting go of these myths opens up opportunities for growth and learning. Financial planning isn't about reaching perfection but rather about making informed decisions based on your current situation and future aspirations. Each step taken toward understanding your finances brings clarity and confidence.

Ready to Reclaim Your Financial Future?

Understanding Your Financial Landscape

Many individuals in their 30s and 40s feel overwhelmed when it comes to financial planning. They often believe they have missed the boat and that it's too late to make meaningful changes. However, this is a misconception. The truth is that it's never too late to take charge of your financial future. There are effective strategies available that can help you get started on the right path, regardless of your current situation or past decisions.

Establishing clear financial goals is the first step toward taking control of your finances. Whether you want to save for a home, fund your children's education, or prepare for retirement, having specific objectives will provide direction. Take time to reflect on what is important to you and set measurable goals with realistic timelines. For instance, if you aim to save $20,000 for a down payment on a house in five years, break that down into manageable monthly savings targets.

Once your goals are established, creating a budget becomes essential. A budget allows you to see where your money is going and helps identify areas where adjustments can be made. Start by tracking your income and expenses for at least a month. This data will help you categorize spending and prioritize needs over wants. With this information, you can create a budget that aligns with your financial goals while still allowing for some flexibility.

Understanding debt management is also crucial for those beginning their financial journey later in life. Many people carry various forms of debt, such as credit cards or student loans, which can be overwhelming. Begin by listing all debts along with their interest rates. Focus on paying off high-interest debt first while making minimum payments on others—this strategy often yields the best results in terms of reducing overall interest paid over time.

Emergency savings should not be overlooked either. Life is unpredictable, and having a financial cushion can provide peace of mind when unexpected expenses arise. Aim to build an emergency fund that covers three to six months' worth of living expenses. Start small; even setting aside $50 per paycheck can accumulate over time and create a safety net against financial shocks.

Investing may seem daunting if you're new to it, but it's an essential component of long-term financial planning. Begin by educating yourself about different investment options like stocks, bonds, or mutual funds. Consider starting with low-cost index funds or target-date retirement accounts, as they offer diversification with relatively lower risk. Even small investments can grow significantly over time thanks to the power of compound interest.

As you gain confidence in managing your finances, consider seeking professional advice from a certified financial planner. A knowledgeable advisor can help tailor strategies specifically for your circumstances and guide you toward achieving your goals more effectively. This partnership can also alleviate the stress of navigating complex financial landscapes alone.

Remember that financial planning is not a one-time event but an ongoing process. Regularly review your progress toward goals and make necessary adjustments based on changing life circumstances or priorities. Flexibility is key; what worked last year may not serve you well today.

By understanding these fundamental strategies—setting clear goals, budgeting effectively, managing debt wisely, building an emergency fund, investing smartly, seeking professional guidance when needed—you empower yourself to take control of your financial future at any age. The sooner you start implementing these practices, the closer you'll be to achieving the financial dignity you've always desired.

Embracing Financial Control at Any Age

Taking charge of your financial destiny can feel daunting, especially if you're starting later in life. However, it's essential to recognize that the power to change your financial future lies within your grasp, no matter when you begin. The first step is to shift your mindset from viewing financial planning as a chore or an obligation to seeing it as an opportunity. Understand that every action you take today can have a significant impact on your tomorrow.

Confidence often stems from knowledge. Educating yourself about financial concepts is crucial. Begin with the basics: budgeting, saving, and investing. There are numerous resources available—books, podcasts, online courses—that cater specifically to beginners. Take time each week to absorb this information. As you learn more, your confidence will grow. You'll start making informed decisions rather than reacting out of fear or uncertainty.

Setting clear financial goals is another vital aspect of this journey. Identify what matters most to you—whether it's saving for retirement, buying a home, or funding a child's education—and establish specific targets. Break these down into manageable steps and timelines. For instance, if retirement is a goal, calculate how much you need to save monthly to reach that target by a certain age. This approach not only clarifies your path but also provides motivation as you track your progress.

Accountability can significantly boost your confidence and commitment to your financial plan. Consider partnering with a friend or family member who shares similar goals; this support system can help keep both of you on track and motivated. Alternatively, working with a financial advisor can provide personalized guidance tailored to your situation. Having someone in your corner can make the process feel less overwhelming.

It's also important to cultivate a positive relationship with money. Many people carry negative beliefs about finances rooted in past experiences or societal messages about wealth and success. Challenge these thoughts by practicing gratitude for what you have and focusing on the opportunities ahead rather than the mistakes behind you. Each small success in your financial planning reinforces this positive mindset.

Recognizing that setbacks are part of the process is equally important. Life happens—unexpected expenses arise, investments may falter, and plans can change. Instead of allowing these challenges to deter you, use them as learning experiences. Reflect on what went wrong and adjust your strategy accordingly without losing sight of your overarching goals.

Lastly, remember that progress over perfection is key in financial planning. It's easy to become paralyzed by the fear of making mistakes or not doing things perfectly right away. Aim for continuous improvement rather than flawless execution. Celebrate small victories along the way; they build momentum and foster resilience.

By adopting these practices and shifting your perspective towards proactive financial management, you'll find yourself taking confident strides towards securing a brighter future—regardless of when you choose to start this journey. The path may have its challenges, but each step forward brings you closer to achieving the financial dignity that empowers you to live life on your terms.

If you've ever thought you were too late to start organizing your finances, let's set that myth aside once and for all. Financial planning is not confined to a specific age; it's a tool available to everyone, whether you're in your 30s, 40s, or beyond. By embracing this mindset, you empower yourself to step confidently into financial management, regardless of your starting point.

Starting your financial planning journey later in life can indeed present unique challenges, but it also brings distinct advantages, such as greater life experience and often more accumulated resources. What's essential is adopting a strategic approach that aligns with your current life stage. Tailored strategies for middle-aged beginners are not just a theoretical concept; they are practical, actionable plans that have proven effective for many who thought it was too late.

One of the most critical steps in taking charge of your financial destiny is developing the confidence to do so. Understand that every step you take builds that confidence. Whether it's setting a budget, planning for retirement, or investing wisely, each action reinforces your ability to manage your financial future. Remember, the goal here is not just to organize your finances but to build a foundation that supports your life's dreams and goals without the burden of financial stress.

The journey towards financial dignity involves continuous learning and adjustment. It requires persistence and the willingness to adapt as your circumstances and the financial landscape change. By starting today, you're not just planning for tomorrow; you're setting the stage for a lifetime of financial clarity and security.

So, take that first step. Seek knowledge, apply what you learn, and gradually, you will transform your financial anxiety into a sense of accomplishment and peace. Your age doesn't define your ability to manage your finances—it's your actions that make the difference. Embrace this journey with optimism and determination, knowing that it's never too late to influence the quality of your future.

Reflection Questions

- **Personal Assessment**: Reflect on your financial situation. What are your current assets, liabilities, and financial habits? How do they align with your goals?
- **Challenging Myths**: What age-related beliefs about financial planning have held you back, and how can you reframe your mindset to focus on the opportunities ahead?
- **Taking Action**: Which of the suggested strategies (e.g., setting goals, budgeting, investing) feels most accessible to you right now? What small step can you take this week to begin implementing it?
- **Overcoming Barriers**: What fears or obstacles have prevented you from starting your financial journey sooner? How can you address or overcome these challenges?
- **Building Confidence**: How can you celebrate small financial victories to build momentum and confidence in your ability to manage your finances effectively?

Summary of Actions to Implement

- **Evaluate Your Current Finances**: List all your assets, debts, and income sources to understand where you stand.
- **Set Clear, Measurable Goals**: Identify financial objectives (e.g., saving for a home, paying off debt) and establish realistic timelines.
- **Create a Practical Budget**: Track expenses, prioritize needs over wants, and allocate resources toward achieving your goals.
- **Start Small with Savings**: Build an emergency fund by setting aside a manageable amount regularly.
- **Learn About Investing**: Research beginner-friendly options like index funds or retirement accounts to begin growing your wealth.
- **Seek Guidance**: Consult a certified financial planner for personalized advice to navigate complex decisions.
- **Regularly Review Progress**: Periodically revisit your plan to make adjustments and stay aligned with your evolving goals.

CHAPTER 14

SET IT AND FORGET IT – AUTOMATING YOUR FINANCIAL SUCCESS

Can Automation Pave the Way to Financial Freedom?

In the quiet hum of early morning, Michael stood at the kitchen counter, his hands wrapped around a warm mug of tea. The sun was just beginning to peek through the blinds, casting long shadows across the floor. He was deep in thought, pondering over his finances, which seemed more like a tangled web than a clear path forward.

For years, Michael had wrestled with managing his money. His job as a freelance graphic designer offered freedom but came with unpredictable income streams that made financial planning feel like navigating through a storm without a compass. The idea of automating his savings and bill payments had crossed his mind before; it was like a beacon in the night that he was too cautious to reach for.

His sister Emily had embraced automation in her financial life years ago. She often shared how it simplified her life, how each bill was paid on time without her lifting a finger and how her savings account grew without her needing to think about it. "It's about setting it and forgetting it," she would say with a smile. But for Michael, giving up that control felt unnerving.

As he sipped his tea, he recalled last month's late payment fee on his electricity bill—an oversight because he was too caught up in a project deadline. It gnawed at him; such mistakes were small but chipped away at his hard-earned money. The room filled with the mechanical buzz of the refrigerator kicking on, pulling him back from his reverie.

Stepping over to his laptop, Michael opened his banking app. His fingers hovered over the keyboard. Could this be the step towards consistency he needed? The screen displayed various options for automation, each one a gateway to potential relief from financial missteps.

Outside, birds chirped as they flitted from tree to tree, their movements seamless and unburdened. Michael wondered if automating his financial obligations could grant him similar freedom—freedom from late fees, from anxiety over unpaid bills, from the relentless mental checklist of dues and don'ts.

He imagined a future where he no longer lay awake at night running through lists of payments due or savings not yet deposited—a future where he could focus more on creating beautiful designs rather than worrying about financial mismanagement.

Is relinquishing manual control over finances truly freeing, or does it merely mask deeper issues of financial discipline?

Unlocking the Power of Financial Automation

In today's fast-paced world, managing personal finances can often feel overwhelming. The complexities of budgeting, saving, and ensuring timely bill payments can lead to stress and anxiety, undermining our quest for financial security and peace of mind. However, there is a powerful tool at our disposal that promises not only to simplify these tasks but also to enhance our overall financial well-being: automation.

Automation serves as a foundational strategy for achieving and maintaining financial dignity. By setting up automatic mechanisms for savings and bill payments, we not only streamline our financial operations but also fortify our discipline in managing money. This approach significantly reduces the likelihood of human error and relieves us from the constant mental load of keeping track of numerous due dates and savings goals.

Embracing Technological Aid for Financial Stability

The primary advantage of automating your financial tasks is the consistency it brings to your financial life. Whether it's transferring a portion of your paycheck into a savings account or paying monthly bills, automation ensures that these critical tasks are completed on time, every time. This methodical approach prevents late fees and penalties associated with missed payments and also helps in building a solid credit score over time.

Furthermore, the psychological relief that comes with automation cannot be overstated. Knowing that your financial obligations are being managed accurately and punctually can free up mental space and reduce anxiety related to monetary matters. This peace of mind is crucial in fostering a sense of financial security and stability.

The Role of Technology in Minimizing Errors

In this digital age, leveraging technology to manage our finances is more accessible than ever. Advanced software and applications not only facilitate automatic transactions but also offer enhanced security features that protect against fraud and theft. By utilizing these tools, you minimize the risk of errors that can often occur in manual handling of finances.

Moreover, technology aids in keeping a detailed record of all financial transactions, providing you with clear insights into your spending patterns and helping you make informed decisions about future investments and expenditures. This level of detail supports better budgeting strategies and financial planning.

Preparing for Long-Term Financial Health

As we explore these facets of financial automation, we aim not just to provide temporary solutions but to foster enduring habits that support long-term financial health. Automating your savings, particularly, plays a critical role in this aspect. It instills a "pay yourself first" mentality, which is essential for building wealth over time.

By adopting automated systems, you're not only ensuring regular contributions to your savings but are also building resilience against economic fluctuations. This proactive approach is key in transitioning from short-term financial survival to long-term financial thriving.

In essence, embracing automation is about making strategic choices today that will pave the way for a financially dignified tomorrow. It's about setting up systems that work tirelessly behind the scenes so you can focus more on living life with less stress about money.

As we move forward in this chapter, remember that each step towards automation is a step towards liberating yourself from the daily grind of financial management. It's about reclaiming time and energy to focus on what truly matters—your personal growth and well-being.

Managing finances can often feel overwhelming, especially when juggling multiple bills and trying to save for future goals. Automating savings and bill payments is a straightforward way to ease this burden. By setting up automatic transfers to your savings account and scheduling bill payments, you can take control of your financial health without having to constantly monitor every transaction. This method not only simplifies your financial life but also helps in establishing a disciplined approach towards managing money.

To get started, first, assess your current financial situation. List all your income sources, expenses, and existing savings. Next, identify how much you can realistically save each month. Once you have a clear picture, set up a dedicated savings account separate from your regular checking account. This step creates a psychological barrier that makes it less tempting to dip into your savings for everyday expenses. Automating monthly transfers from your checking account to this savings account ensures that you are consistently saving without having to think about it.

Bill payments can be another source of stress. Late fees and missed deadlines can quickly add up, affecting both your credit score and overall financial stability. By automating bill payments, you ensure that essential expenses such as rent, utilities, and insurance are paid on time every month. Most banks and service providers offer options for automatic withdrawals or online payment setups. Take the time to review the available options and choose what works best for your needs.

While setting up automation may seem tedious initially, it's crucial to take the time to do it right. Use a calendar or budgeting app to track when payments will be deducted from your account or when transfers will occur. This practice not only helps in avoiding overdraft fees but also keeps you informed about your financial activity each month.

Another important aspect of automation is regularly reviewing your setup. Life circumstances change—income levels fluctuate, bills increase, or savings goals shift. Schedule periodic check-ins (every few months) to reassess your automated processes. This review ensures that you remain aligned with your current financial goals and prevents any surprises down the line.

Incorporating automation into financial management doesn't just save time; it actively fosters discipline in saving and spending habits. When you automate savings, those funds become a priority rather than an afterthought. This shift in mindset transforms how you view money—less as something to worry about and more as a tool that supports your goals.

For those who may feel hesitant about relinquishing control over their finances through automation, it's essential to understand the long-term benefits of this approach. Automation reduces the chances of human error, such as forgetting due dates or miscalculating how much should be saved each month. Furthermore, it minimizes the mental load associated with managing finances manually, allowing you to focus on other aspects of life that matter just as much.

As you embark on this path toward automated financial management, remember that every small step counts towards greater financial freedom. The initial setup may require effort and attention, but it leads to a smoother financial journey ahead.

Ready to Discover the Psychological Benefits of Automating Your Finances?

Understanding the Psychological Benefits of Automation

Many people experience overwhelming stress when managing their finances. The constant worry about bills, savings, and unexpected expenses can create a heavy psychological burden. Automating financial tasks can significantly alleviate this pressure. By setting up systems that handle routine transactions for you, you can free your mind from the minutiae of daily financial management.

Automation fosters a sense of control. When you set up automatic transfers for savings or bill payments, you establish a predictable financial routine. This predictability can lead to reduced anxiety about whether you've remembered to pay a bill or contribute to your savings. Knowing that these tasks are taken care of allows you to focus on other areas of your life without the nagging worry about your finances.

Moreover, automating financial tasks helps eliminate decision fatigue. Each time you need to decide whether to save or spend, you're using valuable mental energy. By automating these decisions, you're effectively removing them from your daily considerations, allowing you to conserve that energy for more significant choices in life. It's like creating a streamlined process for your finances—one that minimizes unnecessary stress and maximizes clarity.

The psychological rewards extend beyond mere convenience. Many individuals find that automation instills a sense of accomplishment and progress. When you see your savings account grow each month without having to think about it actively, it reinforces positive financial habits and builds confidence in your ability to manage money effectively. You are not just saving; you are taking concrete steps toward achieving your financial goals.

It's essential to recognize that automation is not a one-size-fits-all solution; it requires thoughtful setup and regular review. Take the time to assess your income and expenses so that you can create an automated system that works for you. By being proactive in this process, you're not only making life easier but also nurturing an empowering mindset around money management.

Another significant benefit is the reduction of emotional spending. When finances are automated, there's less room for impulsive decisions driven by emotions. For instance, if you've already allocated funds for savings before receiving your paycheck, there's less temptation to spend on non-essentials because you've prioritized what matters most—your future financial stability.

Finally, embracing automation encourages a growth mindset. As you witness the positive outcomes of consistent saving and timely bill payments, you're likely to feel more motivated about tackling other aspects of your finances—like investing or budgeting more effectively. This transformation from feeling trapped in anxiety over money to experiencing empowerment through discipline is profound and life-changing.

In summary, automating financial tasks offers numerous psychological benefits that help reduce anxiety and promote confidence in managing money. By fostering control over your finances and encouraging positive habits, automation transforms how you view money management from a source of stress into an empowering journey toward financial dignity and freedom.

Embrace Technology for Financial Management

Utilizing technology in financial management can significantly reduce errors and enhance consistency. With the right tools, managing your finances can become a streamlined process that requires minimal daily effort. Automated budgeting apps, for instance, help track income and expenses in real-time, allowing you to see where your money goes without manually entering every transaction. This reduces the likelihood of mistakes that often arise from manual calculations or forgotten entries.

Online banking services offer features like automatic bill pay and reminders for upcoming payments. By setting up these services, you ensure that bills are paid on time, which not only avoids late fees but also helps maintain a good credit score. Consider linking your bills to an online banking platform that can automatically withdraw funds when due. This removes the stress of remembering due dates and keeps your financial commitments in check.

Investing platforms have also adopted automation features that make investing simpler. Robo-advisors, for example, provide tailored investment strategies based on your financial goals and risk tolerance. By automating contributions to these platforms, you can invest consistently without needing to actively manage your portfolio every day. This approach not only minimizes errors associated with manual trading but also instills a disciplined investment habit.

Mobile apps designed for savings can further enhance your financial strategy. Some applications allow users to round up purchases to the nearest dollar and automatically transfer the difference into a savings account. This method not only promotes saving but does so in a way that feels effortless. By leveraging technology, you can make saving a natural part of your spending habits without feeling deprived.

Security is another crucial aspect when utilizing technology for financial management. Many modern financial tools incorporate robust security measures such as two-factor authentication and encryption protocols. This ensures that your sensitive information remains protected while you focus on achieving financial stability. Always choose reputable platforms with strong security features to safeguard your personal data.

Regularly reviewing automated transactions is essential for maintaining accuracy in financial management. Even automated systems require oversight to ensure they function correctly and align with your current financial situation. Set aside time monthly to check your accounts, review transactions, and adjust settings as needed based on changes in income or expenses.

Incorporating technology into your financial management not only minimizes errors but also promotes consistency and discipline in handling money matters. By embracing these tools, you shift from reactive money management to proactive planning, which is key to achieving long-term financial goals. The earlier you start utilizing technology effectively, the more control you will gain over your finances, paving the way toward lasting financial success.

Automate to Liberate: A Step-by-Step Guide to Financial Automation

The essence of financial empowerment lies not just in earning money, but in managing it wisely and consistently. By automating your financial processes, you take a significant step towards achieving a stress-free financial life. This systematic approach ensures that your savings grow and your bills are paid on time, all while minimizing the psychological burden and the potential for human error. Here's a practical step-by-step guide to set you on this path:

Step 1: Assess Your Finances

Begin by listing all your regular expenses—including utilities, rent, insurance, and other recurring payments. Understanding what goes out monthly is critical to setting up effective automation.

Step 2: Budget with Precision

Create a budget that clearly allocates a portion of your income to savings and necessities, while also allowing for discretionary spending. This clarity is crucial for setting up automation that aligns with your financial goals.

Step 3: Select the Right Savings Account

Choose a savings account that offers a favorable interest rate and limited access. This helps in growing your funds and discourages impulsive withdrawals.

Step 4: Automate Your Savings

Utilize your bank's online tools to set up automatic transfers to your savings account. Timing these right after you receive your income ensures that saving takes precedence over spending.

Step 5: Automate Bill Payments

Set up automatic payments for all your regular expenses. Align these with your income schedule to avoid late payments and the stress that comes with them.

Step 6: Monitor and Adjust

Use financial tracking apps to monitor your spending and savings. This real-time data can help adjust your budget as needed, ensuring you stay on track.

Step 7: Regular Reviews

Make it a habit to review your financial automation setup every six months. This will help you make necessary adjustments in response to any changes in your financial situation or goals.

By following these steps, you commit to a disciplined and consistent approach to financial management. Automation not only helps in maintaining financial order but also frees up mental space, allowing you to focus on other important aspects of life. As you continue on this journey, remember that each step forward is a step towards greater financial freedom and peace of mind.

Reflection Questions

- What are the biggest challenges you currently face in managing your finances, and how could automation help address them?
- Reflect on a time when you missed a payment or struggled to save consistently. How would automated systems have prevented that situation?
- What fears or hesitations do you have about automating your finances, and how could you address them to make automation a reality in your financial life?
- How can you use financial automation to align better with your long-term goals, such as saving for retirement, paying off debt, or building an emergency fund?
- What specific actions can you take today to start automating your savings and bill payments, and how will you monitor these systems over time?

Summary of Actions to Implement:

- **Assess Your Current Finances:** Review your income, expenses, and savings to understand your financial flow.
- **Set up Automation:** Arrange automatic transfers for savings and automate bill payments through your bank or service providers.
- **Create Dedicated Accounts:** Use separate accounts for daily expenses and long-term savings to create a psychological barrier against unnecessary spending.
- **Utilize Technology:** Leverage budgeting apps or online banking features to track finances and ensure timely payments.
- **Regularly Review Automation:** Schedule periodic check-ins to adjust automation settings as your financial circumstances and goals evolve.

CHAPTER 15

BEYOND BUDGETING – INCREASING YOUR INCOME TO ESCAPE PAYCHECK-TO-PAYCHECK LIFE

Balancing Acts and Unseen Battles

The morning light spilled over the edge of the worn kitchen counter where Michael sat, his fingers tapping a staccato rhythm against the wood. His mind was a whirlpool of numbers—budgets, expenses, potential income from side gigs he'd been considering. The steam from his coffee cup brushed against his face, carrying with it the sharp scent of caffeine that promised alertness but seldom delivered peace.

Outside, the city was waking up; cars murmured along the streets, and pedestrians began their daily dance on the sidewalks. Michael watched them for a moment through the window, each person a story, each story likely knotted with its own financial threads. He turned back to his laptop, its screen glowing with an open document titled "Financial Freedom Plan". It was more of a hopeful gesture than a concrete plan at this stage.

His thoughts wandered to last night's conversation with Sarah. She had talked about her freelance projects with such fervor. "It's not just about cutting costs, Mike. It's about creating more," she had said. Her words echoed in his mind as he reviewed his monthly expenses again. Could he really increase his income by following her path? The doubt nibbled at him like a persistent mouse.

The clock ticked audibly in the background, slicing through his musing and reminding him of the day's demands. He needed to leave soon for his job at the tech store—a job that paid bills but strangled his hours. The thought of negotiating a raise flickered in his mind, fueled by necessity but dampened by anxiety over how such a conversation might unfold.

As he stood to clear his breakfast dishes, Michael felt the cool tile underfoot contrast sharply with the warm sunbeam that now stretched across the kitchen floor. This duality seemed to mirror his current predicament—comfort in routine against the warmth of potential new ventures.

He glanced once more at his financial spreadsheet before shutting down the laptop; numbers still danced behind his eyelids as he grabbed his jacket and headed out into the crisp morning air.

Could stepping into new opportunities truly balance out one's financial equation?

Unleashing Potential: Elevate Your Earnings to Achieve Financial Dignity

Financial freedom is not solely about frugality; it's equally about forging paths to enhance your income. This pivotal concept, often overshadowed by the emphasis on cutting costs, forms the cornerstone of our discussion in this chapter. As we delve into effective strategies for boosting your earnings, remember, the goal is not just to survive financially but to thrive, transforming stress and anxiety into confidence and calm.

The journey towards financial dignity involves a dual approach: meticulous expense management paired with proactive income enhancement. Here, we will explore practical steps to identify and pursue opportunities that can significantly elevate your income. Whether it's through side gigs, freelancing, or climbing the career ladder, understanding how to tap into these resources is crucial.

Exploring Diverse Income Avenues

Firstly, let's consider the landscape of side gigs and freelancing opportunities. The gig economy has democratized income generation, offering flexible options that can be tailored to fit individual skills and schedules. This chapter will guide you through selecting the right gig, setting realistic goals, and effectively managing time between multiple commitments.

Mastering Negotiations and Career Advancements

Next, we shift focus to career advancement. Often, the potential for increased earnings lies within your current career trajectory. Learning how to negotiate salaries effectively or seek promotions can substantially impact your financial status. We'll provide you with key strategies and real-life examples to prepare you for these conversations with confidence.

Balancing Acts: Income Augmentation Meets Expense Management

Lastly, the true art lies in balancing this augmented income with strategic expense management. It's not just about making more money but making every dollar work efficiently towards building lasting financial security. By integrating these practices, you not only escape the paycheck-to-paycheck cycle but also build a robust foundation for future wealth.

Throughout this exploration, remember that each step taken is a move towards greater financial autonomy and dignity. The techniques discussed are not quick fixes but part of a broader strategy designed to transform your financial landscape within 6-12 months. This transformation requires commitment and discipline but leads to a life where money is a tool for achieving dreams, not a source of endless worry.

By embracing both pillars of financial health—increasing income and managing expenses—you equip yourself with the resilience needed in today's economic environment. Every chapter previously has set the stage for this comprehensive approach, ensuring you have the knowledge and tools necessary for this final push towards true financial dignity.

In fostering this balanced perspective on finance management, you are not just surviving; you are setting the stage for thriving. Let's embark on this transformative journey together, stepping confidently into a future where financial stresses are replaced with choices and opportunities—a future where you live with financial dignity.

Increasing your income can be a powerful strategy to break free from the cycle of living paycheck to paycheck. Many people often focus solely on cutting expenses, which is important, but neglecting income growth can limit your financial progress. By exploring various methods to enhance personal income, you can create more breathing room in your budget and reduce financial anxiety.

One effective way to boost your income is through side gigs. These can range from freelance work in your area of expertise to part-time jobs that fit your schedule. For example, if you have skills in graphic design, consider offering services on platforms like Upwork or Fiverr. This not only allows you to earn extra money but also helps you build a portfolio and expand your professional network. If you enjoy writing, consider blogging or offering content creation services. The key is to identify skills or hobbies that can be monetized without overwhelming yourself.

Another avenue for increasing income is career advancement within your current job. It's essential to recognize opportunities for growth that may exist right under your nose. Start by assessing your current role and identifying areas where you can take on additional responsibilities or lead projects. Communicate with your supervisor about your career goals and express interest in professional development opportunities such as training sessions or workshops. Taking initiative not only showcases your commitment but also positions you for potential promotions or raises.

Networking can also play a significant role in enhancing your income potential. Building relationships within and outside of your industry can lead to job opportunities, mentorships, and collaborations that may not be available through traditional job searches. Attend industry conferences, join relevant online forums, and engage with peers on social media platforms like LinkedIn. Remember that every connection has the potential to open new doors.

Investing in yourself is another crucial aspect of increasing income. This could involve pursuing further education or certifications related to your field, which can make you a more competitive candidate for promotions or higher-paying jobs. Alternatively, consider online courses that enhance skills relevant to emerging job markets. Investing time and resources into self-improvement demonstrates ambition and adaptability—qualities that employers highly value.

Additionally, think about passive income streams as a means of supplementing your earnings. This could include renting out property if you own real estate or investing in dividend-generating stocks. While these options require upfront investment in terms of time or money, they have the potential to provide ongoing financial benefits with less daily effort once established.

It's important to maintain a balanced approach when exploring these avenues for income enhancement. As you pursue new opportunities, keep an eye on how they impact your work-life balance and overall well-being. Avoid overcommitting yourself; instead, choose options that align with both your financial goals and personal values.

Creating a clear plan with specific goals will help guide your efforts toward increasing income effectively. Set measurable objectives such as "earn an additional $500 per month from side gigs" or "attend one networking event each month." Regularly review these goals and adjust them as necessary based on what works best for you.

Are You Ready to Take Action?

Understanding Your Worth

Negotiating salary and seeking promotions can feel daunting, especially when you're already stressed about finances. However, recognizing your value in the workplace is a crucial step toward financial stability. It's important to remember that your skills, experiences, and contributions are valuable assets. Understanding this can empower you to take action.

Before entering any negotiation, preparation is key. Research industry standards for your role and experience level. Websites like Glassdoor or PayScale can provide valuable insights into what others in similar positions are earning. Equipped with this information, you can confidently discuss your worth with your employer. If you find that your current salary is below average, this data will be instrumental in supporting your case.

Building Your Case

Next, compile a list of your achievements and contributions to the company. Be specific about how you've positively impacted the team or organization. Use measurable outcomes when possible: "I increased sales by 20% over the last quarter" or "I implemented a new process that saved our department 10 hours a week." This not only demonstrates your value but also gives your employer concrete reasons to consider a raise.

Also, consider timing when approaching these discussions. Schedule conversations during performance reviews or after successfully completing a project. Choosing an appropriate moment increases the likelihood of a favorable response. Your employer will be more receptive if they're already aware of your successes and contributions.

Practicing Negotiation

Practice makes perfect when it comes to negotiations. Role-playing with a friend or family member can help build confidence and refine your approach. Focus on clear communication—articulating why you deserve a raise without sounding confrontational is essential. Use "I" statements to express how you feel about your contributions rather than placing blame or creating demands.

Remember to be open to feedback as well. If an immediate raise isn't possible, ask what steps you can take to make it happen in the future. This shows initiative and willingness to grow, which employers often appreciate.

The Power of Professional Development

Seeking promotions often goes hand-in-hand with negotiating salaries. Investing in professional development can enhance your skills and make you a stronger candidate for advancement within your organization. Consider attending workshops, obtaining certifications, or enrolling in courses relevant to your field.

Many companies offer training programs or educational reimbursement as part of their benefits package. Taking advantage of these opportunities not only boosts your skill set but also signals to management that you are committed to growth. This commitment can play a significant role in future promotion discussions.

Embracing Resilience

It's natural to face setbacks during negotiations or while seeking promotions; not every conversation will lead to immediate success. Maintaining resilience is crucial in these instances. Reflect on each experience and identify what went well and what could be improved for next time.

Additionally, seek mentorship from colleagues who have successfully navigated similar situations. Their insights can provide guidance and encouragement as you work toward enhancing your income through salary negotiations and promotions.

Celebrating Small Wins

Finally, celebrate every achievement along the way—whether it's receiving positive feedback from management or successfully negotiating even a small increase in pay. Recognizing progress keeps motivation high and reinforces the belief that larger financial goals are within reach.

As you continue honing these skills, remember that improving financial circumstances often requires persistence and patience. The journey may be challenging at times, but the rewards of increased income through effective negotiation can lead to greater financial freedom over time.

By focusing on these strategies for negotiating salaries and seeking promotions, you'll not only enhance your income but also boost your overall confidence in handling financial discussions—a vital step toward breaking free from living paycheck-to-paycheck.

Striking a Balance for Financial Growth

Finding the right balance between increasing income and managing expenses is essential for achieving financial freedom. Many individuals focus solely on cutting costs, believing that reducing spending is the only way to improve their financial situation. However, this approach can lead to frustration and burnout. By complementing expense management with income augmentation, you can create a more sustainable and rewarding financial strategy.

Identifying Opportunities for Income Growth is the first step in this balanced approach. There are numerous avenues to explore, such as side gigs or freelance work. Identify your skills and interests—perhaps you enjoy writing, graphic design, or tutoring. Platforms like Upwork or Fiverr offer opportunities to monetize these skills. Even if you start small, every additional income stream can contribute to alleviating financial stress.

In addition to side gigs, consider leveraging your current job for growth. This might involve taking on additional responsibilities or seeking new projects that showcase your capabilities. Look for ways to enhance your skill set through online courses or workshops relevant to your field. Investing time in self-improvement not only makes you more marketable but also positions you for potential raises or promotions.

While pursuing additional income is crucial, it's equally important to maintain a clear understanding of your expenses. Regularly reviewing your budget helps identify areas where you can cut back without sacrificing quality of life. Focus on discretionary spending—those non-essential items that add up quickly. For example, consider preparing meals at home instead of dining out frequently. These small changes can accumulate over time and provide significant savings.

As you work on increasing your income and controlling expenses, it's vital to set specific financial goals. Define what financial security looks like for you—whether it's saving for a home, paying off debt, or building an emergency fund. Having clear goals helps keep you motivated and provides a sense of direction in both earning and spending decisions.

Collaboration with others can also enhance your efforts toward achieving a balanced financial strategy. Discussing ideas with friends or family members who have successfully increased their income can provide insights and inspiration. They may share valuable tips about side jobs they've tried or strategies they've implemented that worked well for them.

Finally, remember that achieving financial stability takes time and patience. Embrace the journey towards financial dignity, recognizing that both success in increasing income and managing expenses contribute to a brighter financial future. Celebrate small victories along the way; every step toward improvement counts.

By actively pursuing additional income while being mindful of expenses, you create a strong foundation for long-term financial growth. With determination and strategic planning, escaping the cycle of living paycheck-to-paycheck becomes not just a possibility but an achievable reality that empowers you to live life on your own terms.

Escalate Your Earnings: A Step-by-Step Guide

Achieving financial freedom is not solely about cutting costs; it's equally crucial to elevate your income. This balanced approach ensures you not only manage your expenses wisely but also enhance your earning potential to escape the paycheck-to-paycheck cycle. Here's a practical guide to help you make significant strides in increasing your income:

1. Assess Your Current Job Situation: Begin by evaluating your current employment scenario. Consider your job satisfaction, the adequacy of your salary, and the opportunities available for career advancement. This introspection is the foundation for understanding where you stand and where you need to improve.

2. Skill Enhancement: Identify the skills and qualifications you lack that are critical for your career advancement. Invest time in acquiring these skills through online courses, workshops, or certifications relevant to your field. This step is crucial as it prepares you for upcoming opportunities and makes you a more competitive candidate in your industry.

3. Showcase Your Achievements: Develop a comprehensive portfolio that highlights your contributions to your current organization. Use quantifiable data to underscore your successes. This portfolio will be a key asset in negotiations for salary increments or promotions.

4. Initiate Salary Negotiations: Schedule a meeting with your manager to discuss your performance and aspirations. Bring your portfolio and research on industry salary standards to the discussion to strengthen your position.

5. Explore Side Gigs and Freelancing: Look into additional income streams that align with your skills and interests. Whether it's freelancing or starting a small business, dedicate a few hours each week to these endeavors to gradually build a supplementary income source.

6. Network and Seek New Opportunities: Constantly network within your industry to uncover new job opportunities or collaborative projects. Staying connected can lead to unexpected avenues that significantly boost your income.

7. Evaluate and Adapt: Regularly assess the effectiveness of these strategies and be flexible in adapting your approach based on what works best for you. The goal is continuous improvement and adaptation to changing circumstances in the job market.

By following these steps, you not only enhance your ability to earn more but also empower yourself with the skills and confidence necessary for financial growth and stability.

Throughout this book, we've explored various strategies to transition from financial anxiety to a position of dignity and confidence. From managing expenses to increasing income, each chapter has equipped you with the tools needed for making informed financial decisions that pave the way for a secure and dignified life.

Remember, the journey towards financial freedom is both challenging and rewarding. By applying these practical steps and maintaining a disciplined approach, you're not just surviving; you're thriving. Here's to living a life beyond financial stress, filled with opportunities and growth!

Reflection Questions

- **Identify Your Skills and Potential Income Sources:**
  What skills or hobbies do you currently have that could be monetized?
  How can you explore side gigs or freelancing opportunities in your area of expertise without overwhelming your schedule?
- **Career Advancement and Negotiation:**
  Are there untapped opportunities for growth or higher income in your current job?
  What steps can you take to prepare for salary negotiations or promotions, and how will you approach these conversations with confidence?
- **Networking and Professional Development:**
  How can you expand your professional network to create more opportunities for income growth?
  What certifications or training programs could enhance your career prospects and earning potential?
- **Setting Realistic Financial Goals:**
  What measurable income-related goals can you set (e.g., earning an extra $500/month from a side gig)?
  How will you track and adjust your efforts to achieve these goals?
- **Balancing Work-Life and Finances:**
  How can you ensure that your efforts to increase income do not negatively impact your overall well-being and work-life balance?
  What strategies can help you integrate income augmentation with smart expense management for lasting financial security?

Summary of Actions

- **Explore Side Gigs:** Research and start a side gig that aligns with your skills or interests, ensuring it fits your schedule and doesn't overwhelm you.

- **Prepare for Negotiations:** Research industry salary standards, compile a list of your achievements, and practice salary negotiation with a trusted friend or mentor.

- **Invest in Professional Growth:** Identify and enroll in relevant training or certification programs, particularly those supported by your employer, to improve your career prospects.

- **Leverage Networking Opportunities:** Attend industry events, engage on professional platforms like LinkedIn, and seek mentorship to open doors for new opportunities.

- **Set and Monitor Financial Goals:** Create a clear financial plan with specific income targets and regularly review progress, making adjustments as needed.

- **Maintain Balance:** Evaluate your time and energy regularly to ensure your income-increasing efforts support your financial goals without compromising personal well-being.

CHAPTER 16

THE POWER OF FINANCIAL LITERACY

Turning Knowledge into Confidence

For many, financial concepts seem like an insurmountable wall—complex, intimidating, and best left to professionals. However, the reality is that understanding even the basics of personal finance can be empowering and life-changing. Knowledge is not just power in this context; it is the key to unlocking confidence and the ability to make informed decisions.

Imagine standing at a crossroads without a map, unsure of which path to take. This is how financial illiteracy feels. But when equipped with even a basic understanding of budgeting, investing, and debt management, each fork in the road becomes an opportunity rather than an obstacle. This chapter aims to demystify core financial concepts and provide a foundation for building confidence and competence.

Understanding the Language of Finance

Financial jargon often feels like a foreign language. Terms like APR (Annual Percentage Rate), diversification, and compounding interest can make even simple discussions seem daunting. Yet, these terms are the building blocks of financial literacy. Learning their meanings and applications is not just beneficial; it is necessary.

Start by defining common financial terms and relating them to everyday situations. For instance, think of APR as the cost of borrowing money, expressed as a percentage, or diversification as not putting all your eggs in one basket. With each concept explained in relatable terms, the fear of the unknown diminishes.

The Role of Education in Financial Empowerment

Education is the cornerstone of financial literacy. This does not necessarily mean formal courses or certifications. Many resources, such as books, podcasts, and online tools, provide accessible and affordable ways to learn. By dedicating even an hour a week to understanding financial principles, you can build a solid knowledge base that pays dividends in the long term.

Take Sarah, for example. A single mother working two jobs, she felt trapped by mounting debt. Through free online courses on personal finance, she learned strategies to consolidate her debt, reduce interest rates, and create a manageable repayment plan. Within a year, she transitioned from surviving to saving, and eventually, to investing.

Financial Literacy in Action: Creating a Personal Plan

Knowledge is most powerful when applied. Begin by assessing your current financial situation. What are your assets, liabilities, and income sources? Understanding where you stand is the first step in determining where you want to go.

From here, set realistic goals. Whether it's building an emergency fund, paying off debt, or investing for retirement, having clear objectives provides direction. Then, use your newfound financial knowledge to craft a plan that aligns with these goals. Remember, even small steps—like automating savings or reducing discretionary spending—can lead to significant progress over time.

Overcoming Barriers to Learning

Financial literacy is not just about gaining knowledge; it is about overcoming the psychological barriers that prevent action. Fear of failure, embarrassment about past mistakes, or simply feeling overwhelmed can inhibit progress. Recognize these barriers and address them with compassion. Remember, every expert was once a beginner.

By committing to learning and applying financial principles, you take control of your financial narrative. Each concept understood and each step taken is a move towards financial dignity.

Reflection Questions

- How do you currently feel about your financial literacy? What specific areas (e.g., budgeting, investing, or debt management) make you feel most confident or uncertain?
- What financial jargon or concepts have intimidated you in the past? How can you begin to simplify and familiarize yourself with these terms?
- What resources (books, podcasts, and online tools) can you commit to exploring to enhance your financial knowledge? How will you integrate this learning into your weekly schedule?
- What barriers, such as fear of failure or past financial mistakes, might be preventing you from taking control of your finances? How can you reframe these challenges as opportunities for growth?
- What is one small action you can take today to start improving your financial situation? For example, could you automate savings, review your monthly budget, or research investment basics?

Summary of Actions

- **Define Key Financial Terms**: Take time to learn essential financial vocabulary, such as APR, diversification, and compounding interest, using accessible resources.

- **Assess Your Current Financial Situation**: Create a clear picture of your assets, liabilities, and income sources to establish a financial starting point.

- **Set Realistic Financial Goals**: Identify specific, achievable objectives like building an emergency fund or paying off debt, and break them into actionable steps.

- **Leverage Accessible Educational Resources**: Commit to ongoing financial education by exploring free or affordable tools like online courses, books, or podcasts.

- **Address Psychological Barriers**: Recognize and confront fears or doubts about financial management, reframing mistakes as learning opportunities.

- **Take Immediate, Small Steps**: Implement manageable actions, such as reducing discretionary spending or consolidating debt, to start building momentum toward larger goals.

CHAPTER 17

BUILDING RESILIENCE

Preparing for the Unexpected

Financial stability is not just about earning and saving; it is about preparing for life's inevitable uncertainties. Emergencies, whether personal, economic, or global, test the strength of financial planning. Resilience is the capacity to withstand these shocks and emerge stronger.

The Importance of an Emergency Fund

An emergency fund is the cornerstone of financial resilience. It acts as a buffer against unexpected expenses, such as medical bills, car repairs, or job loss. Ideally, this fund should cover three to six months of living expenses. While building it may seem daunting, starting small—even setting aside $20 a week—can lead to meaningful results.

Consider John, who faced unexpected medical expenses after a car accident. Thanks to his emergency fund, he avoided going into debt and was able to focus on recovery. His story underscores the peace of mind and security that comes from proactive financial preparation.

Insurance: A Safety Net

Insurance is another critical component of financial resilience. Health, life, and property insurance protect against catastrophic losses that could otherwise derail financial progress. Review your policies annually to ensure adequate coverage and shop around for competitive rates.

Diversification: Mitigating Risks

Diversification is not limited to investments; it applies to income sources as well. Relying solely on a single job or revenue stream increases vulnerability. Explore opportunities for side hustles, freelance work, or passive income sources like rental properties or dividend-yielding investments.

The Psychological Aspect of Resilience

Building resilience is as much about mindset as it is about strategy. Embrace a growth mindset—the belief that challenges are opportunities to learn and grow. Practice gratitude to shift focus from scarcity to abundance, and seek support when needed. Resilience is not built in isolation; it thrives in community.

Reflection Questions

- **Do you currently have an emergency fund?** If so, is it sufficient to cover three to six months of living expenses? If not, what steps can you take to begin building one?
- **How often do you review your insurance policies?** Are there areas where your coverage might be inadequate or where you could find better rates?
- **What is the primary source of your income?** How could you diversify your income streams to reduce financial vulnerability?

- **How do you handle unexpected financial challenges?** What strategies or habits can you develop to approach these situations with greater confidence and preparedness?
- **What role does mindset play in your financial resilience?** How can adopting a growth mindset and practicing gratitude help you face financial uncertainties?

Summary of Actions

- **Start Building an Emergency Fund:** Set a realistic goal and begin saving a small amount weekly, such as $20, until you reach three to six months' worth of living expenses.
- **Review and Update Insurance Coverage:** Examine your health, life, and property insurance policies annually to ensure they provide adequate protection. Research options for competitive rates to save on premiums.
- **Explore Income Diversification:** Identify opportunities for additional income sources, such as side hustles, freelance work, or investments that generate passive income.
- **Adopt a Resilient Mindset:** Embrace challenges as learning opportunities, practice gratitude to foster a sense of abundance, and seek support from community or trusted advisors when needed.
- **Regularly Assess Financial Stability:** Evaluate your financial resilience periodically, identifying potential gaps and addressing them proactively to stay prepared for the unexpected.

CHAPTER 18

ACHIEVING FINANCIAL DIGNITY

A Holistic Approach

Financial dignity is the culmination of knowledge, resilience, and purposeful action. It is about more than just surviving; it is about thriving in alignment with your values and aspirations.

Aligning Money with Values

True financial dignity comes from aligning your financial decisions with your personal values. Reflect on what matters most to you—family, freedom, creativity, security—and let these priorities guide your financial choices. This alignment transforms money from a source of stress to a tool for fulfillment.

Celebrating Milestones

Acknowledge and celebrate progress, no matter how small. Whether it's paying off a credit card, reaching a savings goal, or making a wise investment, each milestone is a testament to your efforts and growth.

Giving Back

Financial dignity also involves contributing to others. Whether through charitable donations, volunteering, or mentoring, giving back fosters a sense of purpose and community. It reinforces the idea that financial well-being is not just individual but collective.

Looking Ahead

The journey to financial dignity is ongoing. It requires continuous learning, adaptation, and reflection. But with each step, the path becomes clearer, and the destination—a life of financial freedom and fulfillment—comes into view.

Reflection Questions

- **What are your core values, and how do they currently align with your financial decisions?** What changes can you make to bring them closer together?
- **What financial milestones have you achieved recently?** How can you celebrate these accomplishments in a way that motivates you to keep progressing?
- **How do you define financial dignity for yourself?** What steps can you take to make this vision a reality?
- **In what ways do you contribute to others financially or through your time and skills?** How does this impact your sense of purpose and fulfillment?
- **What is your plan for continuing to grow your financial knowledge and adapt to new challenges?** How can this ensure sustained financial dignity over time?

Summary of Actions

- **Align Financial Goals with Values:** Identify your most important values and assess whether your spending, saving, and investing decisions reflect them. Adjust as needed to ensure alignment.

- **Celebrate Milestones:** Create a habit of acknowledging and celebrating each financial achievement, whether big or small, to maintain motivation and recognize your progress.

- **Incorporate Giving Back:** Choose ways to contribute to your community or causes you care about, such as donating, volunteering, or mentoring others in financial literacy.

- **Develop a Long-Term Vision:** Define what financial dignity means for you, and establish a roadmap that includes actionable steps toward achieving this goal.

- **Commit to Lifelong Learning:** Set aside time for ongoing financial education to stay informed and adaptable, empowering yourself to navigate future challenges with confidence.

CHAPTER 19

THE LEGACY OF FINANCIAL WISDOM

Financial dignity is not merely a personal journey; it is a legacy that extends to future generations and society at large. By cultivating healthy financial habits, fostering resilience, and sharing knowledge, we create ripples of impact that benefit our loved ones and communities.

Teaching the Next Generation

Passing on financial wisdom ensures that the next generation is better equipped to navigate their own financial journeys. Start by discussing basic financial principles with children in an age-appropriate way, such as saving a portion of their allowance or setting goals for larger purchases. As they grow, they introduce more complex topics like budgeting, credit management, and investing.

Modeling Positive Behaviors

Actions often speak louder than words. Demonstrate responsible financial behavior in your own life to inspire those around you. Whether it's sticking to a budget, prioritizing savings, or making thoughtful spending decisions, your habits set an example that others can emulate.

Building Community Resilience

Extend your financial wisdom to your community by mentoring others or participating in financial literacy programs. Sharing your journey and insights can empower others to take control of their finances and work towards their own financial dignity. Collective resilience strengthens the fabric of society, creating a supportive environment where everyone has the opportunity to thrive.

Creating a Sustainable Future

Financial dignity also involves considering the broader impact of our financial decisions. Support sustainable and ethical practices in your spending and investments. By aligning your financial choices with values that prioritize social and environmental responsibility, you contribute to a legacy that extends beyond your lifetime.

Looking Back, Moving Forward

Reflect on your financial journey and the progress you've made. Celebrate the milestones and lessons learned along the way. Use this reflection as motivation to continue growing and adapting, ensuring that your financial legacy is one of empowerment, resilience, and dignity.

By embracing the principles of financial dignity and passing them on, you create a lasting impact that transcends individual success. Together, we can build a world where financial wisdom is not a privilege but a shared foundation for prosperity and well-being.

Reflection Questions

- How can you begin teaching financial principles to the younger generation in your life, even in small, age-appropriate ways? What steps can you take to make financial education a regular part of their upbringing?

- In what areas of your financial life could you model positive behavior for others? Reflect on one specific habit you could develop that would serve as an example for those around you.

- How can you contribute to building financial resilience in your community? Are there any opportunities for you to mentor others or participate in financial literacy programs?

- Think about your financial decisions and their impact on the environment and society. How can you align your financial choices with your values to support sustainable and ethical practices?

- Looking back on your financial journey, what are some key milestones you've reached that you're proud of? What lessons from these experiences can you carry forward as you continue to build your financial legacy?

CHAPTER 20

EXPANDING HORIZONS

Financial Growth in a Changing World

In a rapidly evolving global landscape, achieving financial dignity requires adaptability and forward-thinking strategies. As economies shift and new opportunities emerge, staying informed and proactive is key to sustaining growth and stability.

Embracing Technological Innovations

Technology has revolutionized the way we manage and grow our finances. From mobile banking apps to investment platforms powered by artificial intelligence, these tools make financial management more accessible and efficient. Explore options that align with your goals, whether it's automating savings, monitoring spending, or investing in diverse markets.

Cryptocurrency, while volatile, has become an area of interest for many. Understanding its risks and rewards can open new doors for those willing to venture into this digital frontier. However, approach such investments with caution, ensuring that they complement rather than dominate your financial portfolio.

Navigating Economic Uncertainty

Economic cycles of growth and recession are inevitable. Preparing for these fluctuations requires a balanced approach. Diversify your income streams, maintain a robust emergency fund, and stay informed about market trends. Educating yourself on macroeconomic factors can also empower you to make informed decisions during uncertain times.

Investing in Personal Development

Your greatest asset is yourself. Investing in personal development—whether through education, skills training, or networking—can lead to greater career opportunities and financial rewards. In a world where industries evolve rapidly, staying adaptable and skilled ensures long-term relevance and prosperity.

Building a Global Perspective

Financial dignity is no longer confined to local economies. With globalization, opportunities to invest, collaborate, and innovate on a global scale have increased. Consider diversifying your investments internationally and learning about global markets to expand your horizons.

Prioritizing Sustainability

The growing emphasis on sustainability presents unique opportunities for financial growth. From investing in green technologies to supporting ethical businesses, aligning your financial decisions with environmental and social values can yield both monetary and societal benefits.

Reflecting and Adapting

As the world changes, so should your financial strategies. Regularly revisit your goals and plans, adapting them to new realities and opportunities. Embrace a mindset of continuous growth and learning, ensuring that your journey toward financial dignity evolves with the times.

By expanding your horizons and embracing a proactive approach, you can navigate the complexities of a changing world with confidence. Financial dignity is not a static achievement but a dynamic journey that grows richer with each step forward.

Reflection Questions

- How can you begin incorporating technological innovations into your financial strategy?
  Are there specific tools, like mobile banking apps or investment platforms, which align with your goals and would make managing your finances more efficient?
- Cryptocurrency can offer new opportunities but also carries risks. How can you approach cryptocurrency investments with caution?
  What steps will you take to ensure they complement your overall financial portfolio?
- What strategies can you implement to prepare for economic uncertainty?
  How can you diversify your income streams and build a solid emergency fund to stay resilient during times of financial volatility?
- In what areas of personal development can you invest to enhance your skills and long-term career prospects?
  What are the most pressing skills or knowledge you should focus on to stay adaptable in a rapidly evolving economy?
- With globalization offering new opportunities, how can you expand your financial horizons?
  Consider international investments or learning more about global markets—how can these opportunities contribute to your financial growth and stability?

CHAPTER 21

MASTERING FINANCIAL COMMUNICATION

Achieving financial dignity often requires collaboration with family members, partners, and even professional advisors. Effective financial communication ensures that everyone involved is aligned, reducing conflict and fostering teamwork.

The Importance of Transparency

Transparency is the cornerstone of healthy financial discussions. Be open and honest about your financial situation, goals, and concerns. Whether you're discussing expenses with a partner or explaining financial priorities to your children, clear communication builds trust and understanding.

Strategies for Collaborative Planning

In households, financial decisions are rarely made in isolation. Encourage family members to participate in budget planning and goal-setting. For instance, holding regular family meetings to discuss upcoming expenses and savings goals can foster a sense of shared responsibility.

With partners, use tools like shared budgeting apps or joint financial calendars to track progress. Agreeing on a set of principles—such as prioritizing savings or minimizing debt—can streamline decision-making.

Navigating Difficult Conversations

Discussing finances can sometimes be uncomfortable, especially when addressing sensitive topics like debt, unexpected expenses, or differing priorities. Approach these conversations with empathy and a problem-solving mindset. Focus on finding solutions rather than assigning blame.

For example, if a family member struggles with overspending, discuss how small changes can align with larger financial goals. Frame the conversation as an opportunity for growth rather than criticism.

Working with Financial Professionals

Collaborating with advisors, accountants, or financial planners can provide valuable guidance. Ensure that these professionals understand your goals and values, and don't hesitate to ask questions or seek clarification. Remember, you are the decision-maker in your financial journey.

Teaching Financial Communication to the Next Generation

Equip younger family members with the skills to navigate financial discussions. Encourage them to ask questions, share their thoughts, and understand the value of collaboration. This early exposure fosters confidence and prepares them for future responsibilities.

Celebrating Financial Wins Together

Recognizing milestones as a family or team strengthens bonds and reinforces positive behaviors. Whether it's paying off a major debt, achieving a savings goal, or celebrating a wise investment, take the time to acknowledge these achievements collectively.

Mastering financial communication transforms money from a potential source of conflict to a tool for connection and collaboration. By fostering transparency, empathy, and teamwork, you create a foundation for lasting financial dignity and harmony.

Reflection Questions

- How can you improve transparency in your financial conversations? What steps can you take to ensure you are being open and honest about your financial situation with family members or partners?
- What strategies can you implement to involve your family members in financial planning? How can regular discussions about expenses and savings goals contribute to a sense of shared responsibility?
- When faced with difficult financial conversations, how can you approach them with empathy and a problem-solving mindset? What are some ways to address sensitive topics without assigning blame or causing conflict?
- If you are working with financial professionals, how can you ensure they understand your goals and values? What specific questions can you ask to ensure their advice aligns with your financial journey?
- How can you teach younger family members the importance of financial communication? What steps can you take to help them develop confidence in discussing finances and collaborating with others?

EPILOGUE

EMBRACING YOUR JOURNEY TO FINANCIAL DIGNITY

As we close this chapter together, not just of the book, but of your old financial narrative, I hope you feel equipped and inspired to embark on a transformative journey towards financial dignity. This isn't just about having enough money; it's about reshaping your life into one where money serves as a tool to fulfill your dreams and needs without the burden of worry, stress, or anxiety.

Throughout our discussions, we've tackled the essential concepts of budgeting, saving, investing, and making strategic financial decisions. These are not merely theories but practical tools designed for immediate application. They are your stepping stones toward a life where financial decisions are made with confidence and clarity.

Key Insights for Lasting Change

Let's briefly revisit the core ideas we explored:

- Understanding your financial landscape is crucial. Knowing where you stand today financially is the first step toward planning where you want to be tomorrow.
- Creating a budget isn't about restrictions; it's about freedom within a framework that you control.

- Saving is not just for emergencies but for future opportunities and security.
- Investing may seem complex, but it's accessible with the right knowledge and mindset.
- Strategic decision-making involves looking beyond immediate gratification to long-term benefits.

Implementing these strategies requires patience and persistence. However, remember that small, consistent actions lead to substantial results over time.

From Insight to Action

To truly benefit from this book, I encourage you to apply what you've learned immediately. Start with a simple budget or review your current financial habits and identify one area for improvement. Engage with online communities or local groups focused on financial well-being. If possible, seek guidance from financial advisors who align with your newfound knowledge and values.

If anything felt unclear or if certain concepts seemed daunting, remember that learning is a process. Each step forward, no matter how small, is progress.

Acknowledging Limitations and Paths Forward

While this guide provides a comprehensive approach to achieving financial dignity, every individual's situation is unique. Personal experiences, economic environments, and unexpected life events can affect one's financial journey. Therefore, continue seeking knowledge beyond this book. The landscape of finance is ever-evolving, and staying informed is key to adapting and thriving.

A Guided Journey to a Flourishing Life

As we close this chapter of our journey together, it's vital to reflect on the essence of what we've explored. This book has been a heartfelt guide aimed at intertwining the strands of well-being and wealth to craft a life that's not only prosperous but also deeply fulfilling.

From the insights shared, you have the tools to apply these principles in your everyday life, whether at home or in your professional environment. The strategies discussed are designed to be actionable and adaptable, enabling you to begin making small yet impactful changes from day one.

We delved into how managing your finances with mindfulness can lead to reduced stress and greater mental clarity. By setting clear financial goals and adopting a disciplined approach, you're not just planning for future wealth but also ensuring current peace of mind. Likewise, incorporating daily wellness practices like meditation or regular physical activity can enhance your emotional resilience, directly impacting your ability to make sound financial decisions.

To encapsulate, remember these core pillars:

- Financial clarity enhances mental peace: Understanding and organizing your finances can significantly reduce anxiety and provide a clearer path forward.

- Physical health is wealth: Regular exercise and proper nutrition are investments in your body's longevity and capability, which in turn support your financial endeavors.
- Emotional resilience fuels financial decisions: Cultivating a strong mental state allows you to handle financial ups and downs with greater poise and perspective.

While this book aims to equip you with valuable tools and knowledge, it's important to acknowledge that every individual's journey is unique. There may be aspects that require further personal adaptation or areas where additional resources might be needed. I encourage you to continue exploring, learning, and adapting the strategies discussed to fit your personal context.

Taking Action for Transformation

Now that you are armed with knowledge, it's time to turn insight into action. Start by identifying one financial goal and one wellness goal to focus on. Perhaps it's setting up an emergency fund or committing to a morning yoga routine. Whatever the goals, write them down, make a plan, and begin taking small steps each day toward achieving them.

Let this not just be reading material but a blueprint for action—a catalyst for change in both your mental well-being and financial health. Remember, the journey towards balance is ongoing; there will be challenges but also significant victories along the way.

A Lasting Impression

In closing, I hope that the pages of this book serve as continual inspiration for you on your path toward achieving balance between wealth and well-being. Remember that each step forward is a step toward a more fulfilled life.

"It is health that is real wealth and not pieces of gold and silver." – Mahatma Gandhi

Let this powerful reminder resonate as you forge ahead, balancing the scales of health and wealth each day, creating a legacy of wellness for yourself and those around you. Here's to flourishing in all aspects of life!

A Call to Action

Now is the time to take control of your financial narrative. You have the tools and insights needed to change how you interact with money—and through it, how you live your life. Let each decision reflect your commitment to living with dignity, free from the chains of financial stress.

Let us part with these words that resonate deeply with our journey:

"Do not save what is left after spending; instead, spend what is left after saving." – **Warren Buffett**

This powerful reminder highlights the essence of prudent financial management—prioritize saving and make mindful spending decisions that support your long-term stability and peace of mind.

Go forth with courage and optimism. Your path to financial dignity is not just a possibility—it's within your reach.